Ho'oponopono
and Family
Constellations

A traditional Hawaiian healing method
for relationships, forgiveness and love

Ulrich E. Duprée

EARTHDANCER

A FINDHORN PRESS IMPRINT

The information in this book is primarily intended for use in developing and promoting personal character and in healing relationships. The guidance offered has been carefully considered and tested and should be used to accompany and encourage your powers of self-healing. It is not a replacement for competent medical advice. For this reason, all the information featured in this book is provided with no warranty or guarantee from the author or the publishers. The author and/or the publishers and their representatives can therefore accept no liability for any personal injury, loss or damage to persons or property. Thank you for buying this book. Andrea Bruchacova and I use part of the profits from books and seminars to support a school project in India that provides children with an education and with food and clothing.

First Edition 2017
Ulrich Emil Duprée
Ho'oponopono and Family Constellations – A traditional Hawaiian healing method for relationships, forgiveness and love

This English edition © 2017 Earthdancer GmbH
English translation © 2016 JMS books LLP
Editing by JMS books LLP (www.jmseditorial.com)
Originally published as *Ho'oponopono und Familienstellen – Beziehungen verstehen, in Liebe vergeben, Heilung erfahren*

World Copyright © 2015 Schirner Verlag, Darmstadt

Cover Design: Murat Karaçay, Schirner,
Photography: Subbotina Anna/shutterstock.com
Layout: Simone Fleck, Schirner
Typesetting: Dragon Design (Elbe/Wendland)
Typeset in Minion
Printed and bound in China

ISBN 978-1-84409-717-3

Published by Earthdancer, an imprint of:
Findhorn Press, 117–121 High Street,
Forres, IV36 1AB, Scotland
www.earthdancerbooks.com,
www.findhornpress.com

Contents

Dedicated to my parents

Divide and connect – part 1

We are all striving to be happy. Sometimes it's not so easy, however – I'm sure that, just like me, you have experienced unrequited love, grief, disappointment and arguments over completely trivial matters. Perhaps there have been times when you simply didn't know how to carry on or felt absolutely desperate. I have been in those situations and I am quite sure you have, too, in one way or another. The circumstances may differ but the persistent, nagging feelings are the same – and we can all free ourselves from them. This book is for you, for those who both give and receive help in life, for those who would like to lead a happy and harmonious life, to forge loving relationships and achieve material and spiritual riches. On the pages that follow, you will find two superb tools that will help you achieve this: family/systemic constellations and *ho'oponopono*, the Hawaiian forgiveness ritual. Armed with these tools, you will be able to clear the stumbling blocks from your path and take one small step closer to your goals.

As an experienced therapist and seminar leader, I would like to show you how you can (1) release all the things that are holding you back in your life and (2) heal your relationships. In this way, you will have the opportunity of becoming more successful in your life; it is only when we have a good relationship with ourselves, with our fellow human beings, with the natural world and with our spiritual origins that we can attain success. Ultimately, our fellow human beings are always the ones who open doors for us.

The key things that you will find in this book – apart from some digressions into the world of social and behavioural psychology – are simple instructions for family and/or systemic constellations, followed by a description of *ho'oponopono*, the Hawaiian family conference. The very terms 'family constellations' and 'family conference' offer a clue to the way both approaches view a person and the challenges that face them – not in isolation, but within the context of their circumstances. At the same time, you will be using practical exercises to learn how you can combine these two approaches – for your own benefit and for the good of the world you live in. Combining individual elements into something even more powerful was an approach championed by the physician, philosopher and mystic Paracelsus (1493–1541) and known as a 'spagyric' (Greek: *spao* = separate and *ageiro* = unite, combine). This method of natural healing calls upon pharmaceutical and therapeutic practices based on very ancient recipes and formulas that have been handed down through the ages – such as the manufacture of salves that develop their healing powers only when certain herbs are combined.

On our journey through the 160 pages of this book, we shall follow the principles of great philosophers such as Socrates and Seneca, who teach us (1) to find out who we are and (2) to be exactly that person. By now, you may have guessed that this book is all about self-awareness; you will discover some things about yourself and they will make all the difference. As every science always has a theoretical and a practical side, I have suggested possible solutions to the exercises presented in this book, and added a few anecdotes and case studies, so you will be able to see and feel concrete results straight away. One small tip: I would advise that you start a kind of workbook, perhaps an A4 notepad, in which you can record your findings; this methodical approach will help to anchor the knowledge you acquire. We will be following the great Ayurvedic teachers, who would always try each treatment on themselves to start with, never on others. So let's get practical!

Knowing is not enough,
knowledge must also be applied;
wanting something is not enough,
you have to take action.

Johann Wolfgang von Goethe (1749–1832)
in: Wilhelm Meister's Journeyman Years

In developing his Psychology of Vision technique, the American psychologist Chuck Spezzano pointed out that everything is connected to everything else in some way or form – everything exists in relation to everything else, hence the core of each problem has something to do with relationships. When I learned this for the first time, the scales fell from my eyes and I realised I had to heal my relationships: with my body, with my parents, with my money – even with my untidy drawers. I stopped seeing myself as a victim of circumstance – instead, I realised that I had an active role to play, despite all the difficulties, and that I possessed 100 per cent of the power I needed to change things. And so for that, thank you, Chuck Spezzano! It is always other people who open doors for us and enrich our lives.

If you don't have much money, or not enough, it's due to a relationship problem – perhaps with your employer, maybe with your clients, or even with the 'liquid energy' of money itself. However, whatever might be the cause, it's also due to a problem you have with yourself. What image do you have of yourself? How do you value yourself? Do you trust yourself? Are you standing in your own way? Do you love yourself enough that you want only the best and are prepared to pay for it? These are all important questions in terms of a relationship. So how are your relationships? With your parents, your profession or your body shape, with your past and future, with the success of your fellow human beings? Or do you prefer not to think about such connections because you find them difficult to deal with and would rather ignore them? Like it or not, if you suppress these questions, they will force their way back up to the surface as if they had a life of their own – you will have to engage with yourself and your relationships sooner or later. I believe that you, as the reader of this book, are among the most intelligent 5 per cent of people – as only this percentage of the population is interested in self-awareness.

Let's go on a journey together with this book and heal all kinds of different relationships. It is certain to be worthwhile – many surveys, including several carried out by Stanford University, have shown that our perception of happiness and individual success depends largely on our interpersonal relationships. In a twenty-year study, the psychologists Arie Shirom, Sharon Toker and Yasmin Akkaly from Tel Aviv University were even able to demonstrate that people with happy relationships in their workplace live longer.* With family constellations and *hoʻoponopono* to help us, we are perfectly prepared to embark on our journey towards happiness. So, let's open the door and go!

* Work-Based Predictors of Mortality: A 20-Year Follow-Up of Healthy Employees, published in: *Health Psychology*, American Psychological Association, 2011, Vol. 30, No. 3, 268–275.

The family constellation

A brief overview

The issue: interview with a client
The exploration: revealing the connections
   that are holding the system back
The solution: moving towards resolution and the visualised
   solution

Many family constellations take place at the weekend and begin with a facilitator (the therapist) inviting people with a particular problem to sit in a circle with a group of up to twenty other interested parties. In the first phase, the therapist asks the person who has raised the issue (the client or 'seeker') to define his or her immediate problem and then goes on to explore it within the context of that particular family situation – possibly across two or three generations. The therapist will ask the client about any particular misfortunes that may have arisen in the family, whether the parents are still alive, the state of the client's relationship with the mother and father, and whether any violent crimes, bereavements or undesired, excluded members of the family are involved. The therapist then selects several people from the group and asks them to take up positions in the room that represent the members of the family. The exercise begins with just a few representatives as we are working with the core of the family – those family members directly involved in the issue. As the representatives settle into their roles during this second phase, 'representative perception' – a phenomenon that is specific to constellations and has a decisive outcome – takes place: the representatives now feel and act like the people they are representing, even occasionally displaying the same behaviour patterns. There is no explanation as yet for how or why this happens, but it allows the conflicts in the relationships and the interconnections in the situation to become apparent. The therapist gradually repositions the participants to bring order into the system. During the third phase, the participants reposition themselves (guided by the therapist) into a formation that resolves and reconciles the issue. In this healing resolution, the representatives stand in a place where love can flow, as it were. Blockages are released, and the 'constellation' of representatives that has produced this healing resolution generally leaves the participants feeling calm, strengthened, relieved and full of hope. Once this formation has been achieved, the client (who has been sitting beside the therapist and monitoring events as a detached observer) takes the place of his or her representative. The client will now similarly experience the reconciliatory state that was the object of the exercise, which is ultimately anchored with small rituals (bows, for example) and healing sentences.

What is a constellation?

A systemic constellation is a way of visualising relationship conflicts with representatives in a space.

'Systemic constellation' is the general term used to describe the method of selecting people from an assembled group who are then positioned within a space and aligned as representatives of members or parts of a system. A 'family constellation' is a way of visualising the prevailing system within a family and is used as a therapeutic tool in phenomenological psychotherapy. The term 'phenomenon' is used because a constellation involves displaying behaviour and experiencing effects whose causes (1) cannot be measured physically and (2) can scarcely be quantified; in addition, (3) each constellation is unique – it cannot be reproduced. Systemic constellations are therefore considered a non-scientific procedure, as 'scientific' indicates that an effect can be predicted and reproduced, which is precisely what *doesn't* happen in these constellations.

During a family constellation, the intuitive positioning of the representatives brings the inner attitudes of the client towards familial relationships and interdependencies out into the open. Like actors on a stage, the representatives in the constellation reveal subtle relationship conflicts that disrupt the natural functioning of the system (in this case the family – although it could equally be a partnership or a company) and prevent people from developing their full potential. The client is able to view his or her conflict and its interconnections from a dissociated perspective (thanks to the representatives) and is able to 'step outside' his or her own person; this makes it easier to identify disruptive or missing elements – and perhaps even find a way towards a solution. A constellation uses the power of perception to reveal connections and provide genuine help in critical life situations.

Case study

Peter, 42, in his second marriage, is desperate and looking for help. His father abandoned the family at an early point and his mother died four years ago. He feels unstimulated at work and yet continually under pressure; he thinks his boss is incompetent and he and his wife have nothing to say to one another at home. Peter feels exhausted, sad and helpless.

The constellation: Peter, the client, sits next to me, his therapist, and initially observes the constellation. From a group of ten participants, we pick five representatives in order of age to represent Peter himself, his mother, his father, his second wife (Monica) and his first wife (Ruth).

Peter's representative stands in the centre of the room and looks ahead and down at the floor (a possible reference to the dead mother). We ask the representative of the mother to stand at the point at which Peter is looking. We next add the father's representative, who intuitively stands to one side, whereupon Peter's representative shifts restlessly backwards and forwards while simultaneously looking powerless. We now ask the representatives of the two

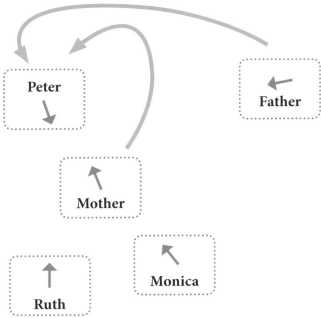

fig. 1

wives to join them, one after the other. Both stand a little to one side, behind the mother (fig. 1).

We ask the representatives what they are feeling. Peter's representative feels feeble and rejected, and has a sense of having been abandoned by his father. Monica and Ruth's representatives feel they are not being acknowledged and that they are unable to see Peter as he is hidden behind his mother; this has even made Ruth very angry. The father's representative would like to withdraw still further from the scene, while the mother's representative is feeling anxious.

The following issues have now been revealed: the father was absent during Peter's childhood and so Peter was exposed to less masculine energy. Peter's shifting back and forth is an indication that on one the hand he rejects his father and yet on the other feels drawn to him as a son. His trust has been disrupted, and his loyalty to his mother binds him to her. His relationship with his mother, who has replaced his absent father, blocks the way to Ruth and Monica. Peter may possibly have unconsciously taken on the role of partner to his mother, and was thus unable to devote himself fully to either of his wives. Whether the mother played an active role in this would be revealed in the later stages of the constellation.

Using small rituals and healing sentences, we now work with all the participants, moving the representatives towards a peaceable (fig. 1) and naturally ordered healing resolution (fig. 2) in three stages. Here, the father and mother stand behind the son and his wife. Monica stands in front of him. In the final stage, Peter takes the place of his representative so that he can feel the supportive power of his parents and make his peace with Monica and Ruth. Monica and Peter fall into one another's arms, ultimately turning to face the front and standing beside one another as a married

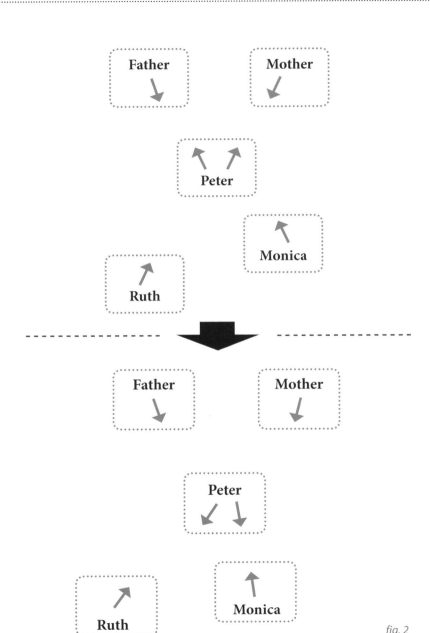

fig. 2

couple. The duration of the entire constellation has been just over an hour.

As Peter reported in a follow-up session about two months later, the original issue, the conflict with his boss, turned out to be a projection (rejection of the father). The family constellation and the reconciliation ritual has resolved this conflict, too; Peter has recognised the competence of his superior and is now using his own skills constructively within the company. He and Monica are taking dancing lessons together in order to grow closer.

The aim of a constellation

To show, perceive, recognise and feel.
To get things moving.
To gain stimulating insights.
To resolve symptoms and causes.

People often feel trapped and robbed of energy in their life situations. They are unconsciously seeking a meaning in life, an individual purpose and a place of fulfilment. At the same time, however, they are so busy that they can't see any way out. Where are you supposed to start? The aim of a constellation is first to identify the (dysfunctional) forces inhibiting the system and the possible causes of difficulties. To be an outside observer of exactly where you are in life can be an extremely intense, perhaps even painful experience, but may provide you with the impetus to take control of your life. Just like clearing a blocked pipe, a constellation can release congested energy. It can lead to momentous insights and give you the courage to solve your problems. Nevertheless, a constellation is not like a pill that you simply swallow, after which you then sit back and carry on as before; you have to want to actively change something.

The important thing is not merely to solve those problems that are immediately obvious, but also to address the underlying causes as precisely as possible – the patterns, traumas from early childhood, entanglements and ancestral programming. Take the symptoms of a physical problem with the body: a painful and recurring inflammation, for example, can be treated and alleviated, but cannot be regarded as healed until the underlying cause is identified and a change – such as a different diet – implemented as a result. It works in exactly the same way in our emotional lives: a serious quarrel may be put aside, but if trauma experienced in early childhood is not resolved, it is only a matter of time before something reopens the old wound and 'presses the red button', bringing the trauma back to the surface. This is why in classic family constellations and *ho'oponopono* family conferences, the objective is to address both the symptoms and the causes underlying the problems.

Calm and the correct 'dose'

During a constellation and in the months that follow, a change takes place on the client's emotional plane that needs time to become established and exert its gentle influence. The client must be in a position to achieve his or her ultimate objective, which is why many facilitators advise allowing several months to pass between two constellations. It is said that power is to be found in peace – and thus in the correct 'dose'. It is not possible to resolve all issues in a single constellation, as if with a magic spell; you work in layers, starting with the obvious (a known quarrel or existential problems, for example) and moving on to the deeper-seated causes. It is like treating a disease for which a doctor prescribes twenty tablets – patients are healed by taking the tablets in the correct dosage. If they take all twenty at once, on the other hand, they will probably receive no benefit at all or may even suffer harm.

How systems are set up

The word 'system' derives from the Greek: *sys* means 'together', while *thema* is strictly translated as 'daily agenda', but more loosely means 'goal' or 'action'. In family constellations, therefore, the elements of a system work together towards a common goal, in a unifying whole. The distinguishing features of a system are order, harmonious interplay and synergetic action. Each of the microscopic living elements in an organism – every individual cell in your body, for example – is a minute, highly developed system in which mitochondria, nucleus, ribosomes and the like work towards a common goal: maintaining life. In so doing, they form higher functional units that include connective tissue, nerves or organs, the cardiovascular system or the autonomic nervous system. Some hundred billion cells combine to form your body. Each of us is a physiological and psychological plurality within a unity, as each individual cell is equipped with consciousness, intelligence and an autonomous spirit: you are in control of some combinations of cells, you can influence others, but many are beyond your control. In the same way, a family is a small system; many families together form a village, then a town and a country – all systems in their turn. Your workplace and your organisation are systems in which people work towards common goals; your car is a system with the objective of getting you from A to B. Everything around you forms systems and relationships, so when you want to change things and become happier or make your life more simple, it is a kind of system optimisation.

The ecosystem and the 'house' we live in

All living creatures on this planet are interconnected; we live in a shared ecosystem. The word 'ecosystem' is derived in part from an Ancient Greek word *oikós*, meaning 'house', and from 'system' (see above), indicating that everything on Earth shares a common agenda. A useful analogy would be to say that we all live in the same house, a house in which the relationships between the individual tenants are extremely complex. The term 'tenant' hits the nail on the head, as this house was not built by any man or animal – it was already in place and available, a fact that sometimes leads the more dominant to consider themselves entitled to live as they please, either through military force or economic power. We all live under the same roof, and when a few behave badly, at first disturbing and then destroying their fellow tenants (animals and plants, the land, water and the air), each one is affected; there is no one living 'outside' the house to keep order and no second house to which we could all move.

Agreeing to live in harmony

Old Hawaiian songs tell the story of how humans once made an agreement with Mother Earth. At that time, the planet was still not as we know it today but was covered with water, the primordial ocean; in order to be granted land, the first humans agreed to look after the Earth, caring for it and safeguarding its living creatures, their brothers and sisters in the animal and plant kingdoms. In return, they received from Mother Earth everything they needed for their lives. This is how the first humans, the ancient Hawaiians and all the other indigenous peoples, lived for millennia – in harmony and in a consensus of giving and taking. In other words, they left no ecological footprint behind them – unlike people today.*

....

* An ecological footprint shows how much space a person uses to maintain his current standard of living. The larger the footprint, the more of the Earth the person uses up. Humans are currently using up the Earth at a rate of 1.5, i.e. the equivalent of 1.5 of the planet's resources. You can calculate your personal 'exploitation factor' on various different internet sites.

Exercise

An exercise about your important and really important relationships

Now let's take a look at the relationship systems involving your birth mother – your own mother – and 'Mother Nature'. Just as every person has a mother who gave birth to them from her own body, Mother Nature gives birth to all living creatures. Our bodies were born of our birth mothers, and the bodies of all living creatures and the elements of all physical bodies come from Mother Nature. They are material (Latin: *materia* = matter, cause, from Latin: *mater* = mother).

Now think about your relationship first with your own mother, and then with Mother Nature, and ask yourself the following serious and critical questions:

What do I love about my mother?
What do I criticise about my mother?
Would my mother have to change for me to be happy?

What do I love about Nature?
What upsets me about Nature?
How would Nature have to change for me to feel better?

Representation is at the core of a family constellation and is usually a method of communication between various levels of existence. Representatives are everywhere in our day-to-day lives: nations are represented at a diplomatic level by ambassadors and ministers, a judge speaks in the name of the people, the icons in Greek Orthodox churches and monasteries are considered direct representations of the saints in heaven. The Old Testament also recounts how the God of the Patriarchs appeared to Moses as a burning bush. When Moses asked if it was the Lord, he received the answer: 'I am that I am.' In the following exercises, we shall refer to an ancient Sanskrit text: the *Bhumi-Gita* (Sanskrit: *bhumi* = Earth, *gita* = song). Here, in the *Song of the Earth* (Bhagavad Purana, Canto 12), the planet uses a calf as its representative to speak to human beings.

Only when the last tree is cut down,
The last river poisoned,
And the last fish caught,
Will the White Man realise
That you cannot eat money.

Cree Indian proverb

Exercise

Reference systems, representatives and proxies

First, read through the exercise and make sure you fully understand what you have to do, which is to

(1) feel, (2) visualise, (3) feel and (4) think carefully.

In the appendix you will find two lists of feelings – choose the two terms that best describe your current emotional state. How are you feeling right now?

In the Ancient Indian *Bhumi-Gita*, the Earth takes on the form of a calf to speak to humans. Now close your eyes, and, for about a minute, imagine the Earth in the form of a calf standing around three metres in front of you. Take a good look at this small calf and be aware of its energy. Open your eyes, search the lists of feelings in the appendix and find the two terms that now best describe your emotional state. What has changed? Once again, close your eyes and visualise the Earth as a calf standing about three metres in front of you. Now bow slowly and respectfully to the calf.

Open your eyes slowly, and now check the lists of feelings in the appendix for the terms that describe your new emotional state. What is the difference between the three emotional states you experienced before, during and after the exercise?

Our common goal

The cosmos is harmony

Our cosmos (Ancient Greek: *kósmos* = order, harmony) is the largest system we know, the great unity. Our universe (Latin: *unus* and *versus* = turned in on one) is a single, glorious symphony in which everything is reflected in everything, like a hologram, and whose totality can be recognised in each part. You are probably familiar with the anatomical topographical maps used in foot reflex zone massage or iridology, in which the entire body is represented within a foot or an eye. Each human body, the mesocosmos, reflects the principles of megalocosmic order, just as a flower or a mountain does.* Musical scales correspond to the spacing and orbital times of the planets, for example, and although an atom is clearly not a solar system, it has a similar structure. This cosmic echo, introduced to European thought by the Ancient Greek philosopher Pythagoras (570–510 BCE), is also known as the *quadrivium* (Latin: four ways) and its aim is to recognise the fundamental value of beauty, harmony and wholeness in everything. The cosmos is harmony and order.

Common goals and common values

Everything in a system works towards one goal. When people lose sight of this goal, it creates disunity and disharmony, and the members of the system become discontent. This is what happens when there is a lack of communication – in a family, a company or an

....
* The triad of micro-, meso- and macrocosmos was part of the teachings of Pythagoras' school of philosophy. The microcosmos is the level of small things such as atoms, microbes and insects, the mesocosmos relates to the level of the human body, and the macrocosmos is a description of Nature. There is also the megalocosmos, a notion coined by the philosopher and composer Georges I. Gurdjieff (1866–1949) to refer to the entire universe with its galaxies, stellar nebulae, pulsars and black holes.

organisation, for example – and the needs of the individuals involved are not respected. By the same token, dissatisfaction can also be the beginning of important changes – you often only learn to appreciate health when you are sick, or a good relationship when it is gone. This is known as the 'goldfish phenomenon': just like a goldfish that only appreciates its life-giving water when it is taken away, and is blind to the obvious and amazing opportunities in life, we have lots of good things around us and yet still tend to complain. Even if 99 per cent of life is running along really well, people still concentrate on the problematic 1 per cent ('focus of deficiency'). We remember what hurts, and this memory can bring insight and personal growth – which is exactly what we are looking for in a constellation.

A good example is in companies where (1) there is a lack of constructive communication and (2) a lack of recognition of the common goal. The American corporate consultant Brian Tracy, who is hired by such companies as an advisor for strategic corporate analysis and planning, has invented an interesting game called *Keep your job*. He asks the manager of a company: 'What do the people immediately below you do in the company? What do you expect of them? What are their primary daily, weekly and monthly duties?' He then goes to the people on the next management level down and asks the following questions: 'What are your duties? Do you know what is expected of you? What are the aims of your company?' The answers of both groups are then compared, and the discrepancies between the results are usually quite startling. Besides their financial corporate goals, I recommend that companies always make a point of setting out their conceptual values as intellectual components of a *mission statement* and/or corporate philosophy: 'What do you stand for as an individual, and what does your company stand for? What is the spirit that breathes life into your organisation or your company?' In the event of any disharmony, this list of shared values makes it easier for the workforce to rediscover their common denominator. This kind of communication is also important in a family, of course – you may well know someone who is a source of problems because something is not being discussed openly in the family.

An exercise that can change your life

Ask yourself the following questions:

Does my family have shared values and goals?
What do I/we think is important?
Where do I/we want to be in five years?

Get your partner, children or even your parents on board and write down a list of values and goals for your family. Write a heading, perhaps something like: 'We think this is important.' You could even turn it into a game one evening, with everyone taking turns to speak, or you could add something to the list on particularly happy occasions, such as on holiday. Then frame your list and hang it in a place of honour. It will bring you much joy and great benefit – I guarantee it!

The four buffaloes – a tale of individual responsibility and family unity

Once upon a time, there lived four buffaloes in a land that is not so very far away. They would make their way majestically through verdant grazing grounds, and as they chewed, they would move their magnificent heads and mighty horns from side to side through the grass. However, whether grazing or sleeping, they were always close together, forming a cross shape as each looked out in a different direction. Occasionally a lion would come by (lions are always looking to hunt down buffalo). 'That would be a fine feast for my family. Everyone would eat their fill – and the vultures can have anything we don't manage!' said the lion to itself as it crept closer on the hunt. Day after day it tried its luck, but no matter on which side it chose to attack the buffaloes, it would always find itself facing their sharp horns – each buffalo protected the others. News of the way the buffaloes stood together soon spread and there was not a lion or hyena that dared come near them. Many years passed, and the four buffaloes – perhaps because they had become arrogant, or perhaps because they had succumbed to temptation, or just out of boredom, nobody knows – abandoned their protective formation and went their own ways. One after the other, they all fell prey to the lions.

A single link that breaks in a great chain
will destroy the whole chain.

Johann Wolfgang von Goethe (1749–1832)
in: Wilhelm Meister's Journeyman Years

Every member of a community is important, as they would otherwise not be there. Nature has given us each of our organs because each is important and necessary. The eyes don't say to the feet: 'We're at the top and we don't need you.' In the same way, everything in a car is in its right place, and no one removes the dashboard lights because they don't like the way they glow. Everything is important, and if there is a problem, it affects both the individual and the group – just as in the example of the four buffaloes.

Reaching the goal more quickly – or: a little order never hurts

Imagine if the brake pedal and the accelerator were suddenly swapped over in your car but no one told you about it. Then imagine if a vital organ such as your liver suddenly no longer knew what it was for and decided that from now on it would prefer to be a brain – best of luck! Or what about this: when you set the table, do you put your knife and fork beside the plate or underneath? As you can see, a little order makes life pleasant and manageable. Order eliminates nasty surprises and without it there would be no websites, no books, no houses, and businesses might just as well shut up shop. Organisational principles make a system efficient and are important for our survival as well, as 95 per cent of our lives is managed by the unconscious. We live according to habits and our lives would be incredibly complicated if we had to constantly think and work stuff out from first principles.

Many relationship conflicts arise because there is no order in a system and/or something is not in its right place. The family members don't know where they belong and have no idea what enormous potential they have, and precisely because people think so little of who they are, there are many who would like to be someone else. It is important to distance yourself from bad things, to get away from negative feelings; they rarely lead to anything good.

Exercise

An exercise for personal system optimisation

Over the next couple of weeks, make a list of all the systems you have noticed around you. Concentrate in particular on looking at your role within these systems and ask what goals you have in common. It's a good idea to use your notebook for this – draw four columns on a blank page and head them: (1) System, (2) Subject, (3) Goal and (4) My role.

Think about your goals, the roles you play and the relationships you have. Working out what you really think about these is the first step towards healing, order and personal success. You might begin by simply clearing out some metaphorical messy drawers, or tidying the basement (your foundations), or even making a start on the attic (to think straight, creating order 'at the top'), or perhaps by sorting out something you have been putting off for ages. I am sure that two weeks later you will find you have made giant strides and brought order to many aspects of your relationships. You will be living more efficiently after ditching so much useless baggage. Travelling light is famously easier.

When you reach the other shore,
leave the boat behind.

American proverb

The elements of a constellation

Client and focus

The client comes to the therapist with an issue. As elements other than people can be represented in systemic constellations, the subject of a constellation is also called the 'focus'.

Case study 1

Nicole is a client and has not seen her daughter for two years. Nicole is at the centre of the conflict and is thus both the client and the focus.

Case study 2

Bernard owns a service provider company in Birmingham. More and more people are taking time off for ill health in his sales department. Bernard is the client and his firm is the focus that will be set up as a constellation.

The therapist

The word 'therapist' is derived from the Greek word *theràpon* and means something like 'servant', 'attendant' or 'companion'. In the Ancient World, the term primarily applied to Asclepius, the god of healing. Therapy was considered a kind of caring and a service in harmony with the gods, and the therapist was a servant of the divine. The facilitator is correspondingly not a healer or saviour but always a companion and servant who uses his or her knowledge and experience to lead the way for clients. A good facilitator should be able to (1) achieve a sense of safety and security and (2) impart a sense of safety and security. Both of these abilities develop as you become more competent, working through your own issues, acquiring personal experience and grounding, and trusting in something higher, the Source of all things or (traditionally) in God.

Impartiality

Impartiality is always required of a therapist in interactions with a client. Compassionate neutrality prevents a facilitator from falling into a saviour role and getting caught up in any kind of perpetrator-victim-saviour complex. As soon as the facilitator makes a judgement in a constellation, he or she is immediately entangled and becomes a subject with their own issues. To pass judgement is to exclude, and what has been excluded is precisely the element that requires attention in a constellation; it needs to be properly acknowledged and then reaccepted.

This doesn't mean that the therapist cannot have issues of their own, however. Everyone has them, whatever their position in life. All it means is that the therapist's own issues cannot become part of a constellation. The facilitator acts as a kind of pilot through uncharted waters for all involved, possessing a certain sense of safety and security in order to be able to impart a sense of safety and security. Despite this guiding role, a good facilitator is not a 'leader'. Instead of trying to control every situation, he or she gives a constellation space. They put themselves in the hands of a higher guidance that you might recognise as 'intuition', 'gut feeling' or 'inner image'.

The issue, information and essentials

When it comes down to it, people are always entangled in various problems and spend much of their time sorting something or other out. The word 'problem' is derived from the Ancient Greek word *próbl ma* and describes how the immortal gods strew *(blema)* stones before *(pro)* us. If such a stone blocks our way (Hawaiian:

37

Ala nou ana), mortals will choose which path to follow – while some complain and fixate on the obstacles, others will use the opportunity to grow through these challenges.

It sometimes seems to me that we unfortunate Western Europeans find ourselves in a crisis every three months. There are problems at work, relationships worries, financial cares, existential woes and apprehension about the future, sickness, trauma and damage in early childhood, family issues, unsettling news in the media, the concerns of others, environmental pollution and the state of world affairs – from this perspective, life does indeed resemble a seemingly endless series of difficulties that begins at birth and ends only with death. A client can seek help with all of these (and much more besides) to find the end of the thread in the Gordian knot of their existence.

A therapist should always listen closely to what the client is saying. The way he or she describes the problem concerned will already be helping to solve it. The therapist should see the young boy within the man, or the little girl within the woman – he or she is a seer, as everything is contained in this moment of *now*: the past has made us what we have become, and we decide every second what we want to make of that in the future – we have no other ingredients, but it's already enough to make a personal success of life. When all's said and done, where you came from is irrelevant – all that matters is where you're going.

It is said that you need a certain level of psychological pressure for a problem to be resolvable in a constellation, and a clear formulation and understanding of the issue is certainly beneficial; it is difficult to find a solution for clients who are only able to describe their problem by 'beating around the bush'. In presenting the problem, they should try to get to the heart of the matter, and a preliminary discussion is useful for reaching this point. A family constellation deals with essentials, after all: birth, life and death, father and mother. It gets down to our closest relationships and earliest experiences. It is about love that has not been received, could not have been given or was even refused. It is about destiny, crimes of violence, war, hunger, sickness, deaths in the family, abortions and adoptions, marriages and divorces.

The causes of our problems as adults lie in the experience we have had with our families, as we are not alone in the world – the links in our destiny are always entangled with those of our ancestors.* Our inner conflicts from our childhood are brought forward into the present, where they are lived out until the issue is resolved. The inner child brings the trapped memories to the surface in the here and now as it looks for healing.** Life asserts its right to happiness at every moment, and your workplace and relationship will seem entirely acceptable stages on which to manifest itself.

The life unexamined is not worth living.

Plato (428–348 BCE)

* See chapter '*Aumakua* – the ancestors', p. 109.
** See chapter '*Unihipili* – the lower self, subconscious and inner child', p. 121.

Exercise

An exercise to find what is really essential

Take your workbook and turn it to landscape format. Draw a horizontal line across a new page. Draw a circle at one end and do the same at the other. The circle at the beginning symbolises your birth and the other circle your physical end.

Now ask yourself where 'today' is and mark it on your timeline. Look carefully at this picture and be aware that your time on Earth in your physical body is limited.

Now write in all the important events that have made a deep impression on you and had a strong influence on your life (Sanskrit: *samskāra*). Decide in each case whether you felt the event had a positive or a negative influence.

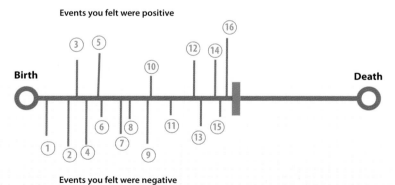

fig. 3

Now pause to take stock, and find the connections between the past and the present, asking yourself in particular which past negative events have resulted in clearly positive outcomes in your life.

Having taken this analytical journey through your past, you deserve a reward: sit up straight, take three deep breaths, smile and say with joyful expectation: 'This is the first day of the rest of my life.'

You should live now as you would wish to have lived when you die.

Marcus Aurelius (121–180 CE)

The group, the 'field' and the representatives

Family constellations often take place at the weekend, with several clients and representatives meeting to address their issues together. Such a 'group' (as they are known in family constellations) forms the 'field', an energetic space in which representative perception becomes possible. After one of the clients has (usually briefly) presented his or her issue, the participants take a moment to reflect; this is a period of silence in which each one connects with the higher power that is the source of what happens here.

The representatives stand in as tokens for the elements of the system. Only they will enable the therapist and the client to recognise dysfunctional relationships. The representatives' openness to feeling what becomes apparent plays a role in the success of a constellation. When taking up a position as a representative, stand up straight, perhaps flexing your knees slightly, with eyes closed and breathing gently, and simply search your feelings. If nothing comes, that's fine, as the inability to feel something is often a sign of defensive programmes that are seeking to protect us against recurring pain. Avoid playing a role (a father, mother, son or daughter, for example) where you know exactly how it would feel to be in this or that situation – doing this means you are merely interpreting the issue and not actually feeling it. A further problem arises when feelings are *thought* (that is, when the representative *believes* or *thinks* that he/she is furious now) rather than actually *feeling* the fire, the anxiety, the waves and the heat in their body, hands and arms, in their back or in their lungs.

As representative, you are a medium and, as such, you empty yourself – until you are completely empty. You can't fit any more liquid into a glass already filled with green smoothie, you can only pour something into an empty glass.* If we are full of feelings, there is hardly room for anything else – but on the other hand, if we were entirely without feeling, our lives would be really empty. This is why relationships are not lived, they are felt. We sometimes find it difficult to identify and put a name to our own feelings, however. There are two lists of terms in the appendix to help you describe your feelings exactly, and you will find these useful for your exercises.

Exercise

An exercise in feeling your own relationships

Visualise some of the people in your life and examine your feelings about your relationship with them. What do you feel? Note down these emotions in your workbook. If they are negative, make a note of what you would like to feel instead in each relationship. Create the following columns in your workbook: (1) Person and relationship, (2) Current feelings about this person, (3) The feelings and relationship you would like. Having defined where you are and where you want to be, you can ask yourself what you would like to do to actively improve your relationships.

* The words 'full', 'fill' and 'feel' are etymologically connected. The verb 'fill' is derived from Old English *fyllan*, 'full' relates to OE *fyllu*, and feel is derived from OE *fēlan*. All these words are related to Fulla, the steward of the treasure chests belonging to the Germanic mother goddess Frigg.

The constellation – practical work with floor anchors

Having completed these productive preliminary exercises, we now move on to an important method for working with systemic constellations, to which we will return several times in the course of this book: the placing of 'floor anchors'. A floor anchor is an object (a sheet of paper or a stone, for example) that you arrange on the floor to represent an object or person within your constellation.* You can work alone using this method (in your sitting room, office, garden or at the beach, with no therapist or observers), collecting experiences and thus rapidly bringing your inner images to the surface and achieving clarity. The easiest approach is to use loose sheets of A4 paper on which you can write appropriate captions.

Preparation

Take five sheets of paper and write one each of the following words on the first four: (1) Me, (2) Father, (3) Mother and (4) Neutral observer. Taking the motto 'less is more' to heart, the aim of this exercise is to introduce you step by step to the procedure used in systemic constellations. Too many floor anchors just complicate matters, which is why you are grouping all your brothers and sisters on one sheet (5). If you have only one sibling, write 'Brother' or 'Sister' as appropriate. If you have more than one brother, write 'Brothers', if you have several sisters write 'Sisters'. If you have a mix,

---

* On Bali, Dr Diethard Stelzl showed my wife, Andrea Bruchacova, and me the tradition that has been handed down of drawing your own body in the sand and then placing stones as representatives for each organ; this helps you to get in touch with your own body in meditation. If you are interested in these and similar methods, I recommend Dr Stelzl's books and his seminars, which are held both on Bali and in Germany, e.g. at the Lichtquell seminar hotel in the Black Forest.

write 'Siblings'. If you are an only child, you won't need this sheet, of course. At the end you will have four sheets if you are an only child, or five if you have siblings. Draw an arrow on each sheet of paper to show the direction of each family member's gaze.

So what happens if you don't know one or both of your parents? What if someone is no longer living? What if you live in a stepfamily and your siblings are from different marriages?* As you can see, it is a good idea to have thought about all this beforehand – as ever, proper planning prevents poor performance later. We should ask ourselves: who exactly belongs in the system? Is everybody allowed in, or does someone have to wait outside? What happens to those who are brought inside, and how do the ones we have left out feel? Who is in which place? Does everyone have equal rights? Who would walk through the door first, or would they all scramble through at the same time – and if so, where would they go? How does each individual feel? And how does the family look when viewed from the position of the neutral observer? These are all things we are hoping to find out.

Constellation, Act 1 – initial arrangement

Find a quiet place where you won't be disturbed for the next hour. Arrange the sheets on the floor however you like, but stay within an area no greater than 12 m². The arrows showing which way people are looking and the layout of the space will help you decide what you feel about the relationships between the family members. Just use your intuition as you work and trust your feelings. Ask yourself if something feels right. Make corrections until the picture accurately reflects your current family situation for you. Remember that this is not about arranging it how it should be, but how it is – this is the

---

* Take a look at the chapter 'The family', p. 51, for how to find answers to such questions.

only way to bring your inner image to the surface, and this is what we want to work with. Now draw the layout in your workbook; it might look like this, for example:

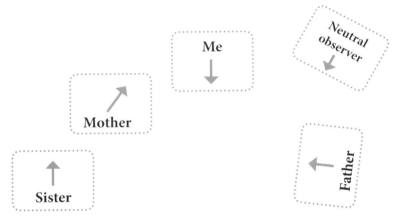

fig. 4

Make a table with four columns so you can make a note of changes in your feelings as the constellation moves: (1) Name, (2) Initial arrangement, (3) In movement, (4) Healing resolution. Write down each name in the book and then concentrate on each sheet and the direction of its gaze. Search your emotions and make a note of your first perceptions, thoughts and feelings in column (2) Initial arrangement.

Constellation, Act 2 – movement

Now do the following: first, introduce some movement and dynamics into your system. The aim of this stage is to see and experience how other people feel when the relationships in the room change. To do this, deliberately place a sheet in an unexpected place and see how it feels to stand there. This step is important for identifying the changes in your emotional body as soon as the relationships in the room change. Now rearrange some other sheets and see how the new positions feel. While standing on a sheet, ask yourself the following questions to check your reactions: how does your father or mother feel, and how do you feel yourself, if you stand a long way off or very close to individual people? How do the relationships feel? Does someone take over control through the changes in the room? Who feels their position reinforced and who is weakened, and in which places? Here too, you can make use of the two lists in the appendix to explore your internal and emotional life and describe your innermost feelings.

To close the session, go and stand in the position of the neutral observer. From here, you can scrutinise your family and each individual member without getting involved in problems. How does this impartial observer view the scene? What do you feel about your family from the observer's position? What touches you? What insight does it bring? Do you see your relatives in a new light? Having experienced the roles of the representatives in this stage, we shall now turn to a formation that will bring clarity.

Constellation, Act 3 – clarification and resolution

In finding the healing resolution formation, we want to move towards an arrangement in which every person is standing in a place that is stronger for them, where reconciliation of conflicts can take place and love can flow between everyone. But how do you find out how your relationships can be moved towards an improvement? Stand in your own position (Me). Ask yourself where your father and mother would have to stand so that love can flow. Now ask yourself the following non-hypothetical question: what would love be doing now? Proceed with empathy, calm and trust, following your heart, and bring your heart and your head into accord. When you have moved a floor anchor, go and stand in the new position to get feedback from the new arrangement.

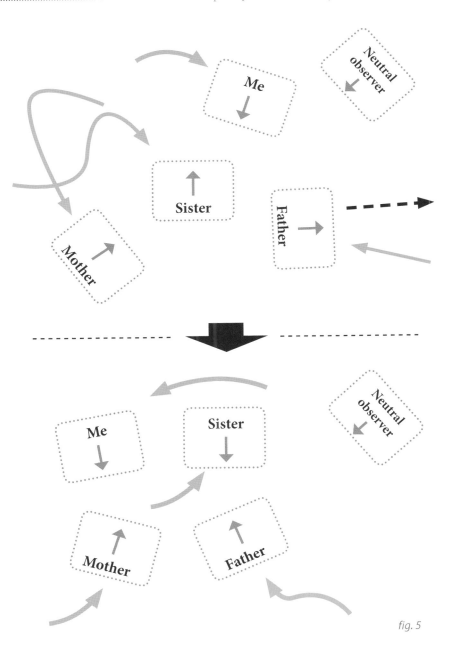

fig. 5

Ultimately, every member of the family will be standing in an emotionally stronger position in the healing resolution you have arranged. Emotions such as goodwill, understanding, helpfulness, self-confidence or joy that you feel in these positions are hints that you are heading in the right direction. Search your feelings in each individual position, reflect on the new arrangement and note your thoughts in your workbook. Fig. 5 will help you to orientate yourself and shows an idealised healing resolution.

Your healing resolution is a wonderful achievement – you have taken the initiative to give yourself and your family more love, harmony and peace. Thank you.

Other factors

The family

Your birth family and/or family of origin

The term 'birth family' and/or 'family of origin' describes the client's direct descent – their blood relatives and ancestors. The inner effective radius of a family constellation will include three generations: the client and any siblings, the parents and the grandparents. Some facilitators also include step-parents and adoptive parents here.

Your birth family includes you yourself, your parents, your siblings and half-siblings, any aborted or stillborn children (including any that have been 'hushed up'), your parents' siblings, your grandparents, great-grandparents and all their siblings.

Exercise

An exercise about your own birth family

Make a family tree of your birth family that goes back as far as your grandparents. Note down each date of birth and date of death where applicable, as well as the profession of each family member and what has become of them.

Your present family

Your present family includes all the people with whom you share a connection because you live with them, you are married to them and/or you have children with them. This includes you yourself, your partner, all your children (including any children from earlier relationships that you have not told your current partner about), any grandchildren, any aborted or deceased children as well as all your earlier partners.

Case study 1

Monica has a son, Michael, from an earlier relationship with Peter. She has been married to George for two years and was expecting twins, but lost these in the third month of pregnancy.

She has asked for a constellation for her present family. There are six people involved: Monica, Peter, Michael, George and the twins. The illustration below shows the final image of the constellation with arrows showing the various connections to indicate the relationships in the present family.

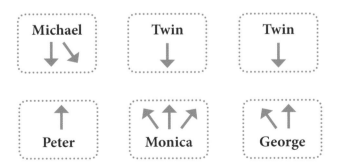

fig. 6

Case study 2

Mike and Gina have been living together for eight years but have had no children together. Gina brought her daughter Lisa (from her first marriage to Joseph) into the relationship. Mike has a son, Richard, who lives with his mother, Anna. Anna and Mike were never married.

Gina's present family consists of Mike, Lisa and Joseph.
Mike's present family consists of Gina, Richard, Lisa and Anna.

Other people

In addition to your birth and present family, there may be other people who influence the system and so will also belong in a family constellation. These might be people to whom you have a special obligation or individuals or groups of people who have had a decisive influence on the fates of the family – for example, victims and perpetrators of crimes (of violence), people leaving or receiving legacies who are not members of the family, company staff, people in a position of power (if someone has lost possessions as a result of the political situation, for example). Our extended 'present system' also includes line managers, colleagues, clients, friends, neighbours, teachers and fellow students – in other words, all the people who influence our lives.

Order and sequence

The important thing to understand with systems, and with families, is that all participants have equal rights – everyone has the same right to live, thrive and survive. However, in parallel with these equal rights is the principle of order and sequence. Here is a simple image to demonstrate this: a small family, consisting of father, mother and child, is sitting in their hut when they hear a commotion outside. Who is the first to go out and check that everything is all right, and who stays with the child? The natural answer to this question rests on order and sequence, and has nothing to do with comparative ego-related terms such as 'better' or 'more important'. This conceptual order takes on a practical dimension when it comes to survival of the species: women and children first!

In family constellations, you will be working with small rituals (bowing, for example) and healing sentences, the precise, clear and unambiguous formulation of which makes them so effective. To bring order into a system, the following sentences may be spoken aloud, for example:

I am your father. You are my daughter/my son. I am older. You are younger.
I am your mother. You are my daughter/my son. I am older. You are younger.
This is your grandmother/your grandfather.
This is your daughter.
This is your son.
You are my father. I am your daughter/your son. You are older. I am younger.
You are my mother. I am your daughter/your son. You are older. I am younger.

Speaking and hearing these sentences helps clients to distance themselves from a possible lack of orientation (Who am I? Where do I belong?) and any associated powerlessness while moving them towards their natural strengths.

There's another example of this topic of order and sequence on your desk: your computer only shuts down when (1) all your documents have been saved and closed, (2) all the programs have closed and (3) the operating system has shut down. None of the programs will work without an operating system and you can't edit a document without a keyboard. It's essential to realise this fundamental principle: there is an order, but at the same time everyone has the same right to existence. In any firm, for example, there is the management, the workforce, particular products or services and customers – no single element can exist without the others, but some sit behind the desk and others in front of it.

To gain a better understanding of what underlies this principle, it is a worthwhile exercise to take a look back at our developmental history. Many hundreds of thousands of years ago, our ancestors lived in caves – and not just when it was raining. Perhaps people just used to stare into the fire in those days (like we do now with the television). The men went hunting while the women and children looked after the fire in the centre. The concepts and ideas of 'mother' (Latin: *mater*), 'matter' (Latin: *materia*), 'earth', 'cave', 'fire', 'oven', 'centre', 'return', 'preservation', 'life and death' are all associated with this archaic image of femaleness. We are born of dust, and to dust we shall return. The female principle is introverted; it is the principle of protecting and preserving, of creation, of bearing children – think of the arc of a dark sky, the Great Mother and the Eternal Mother from which everything comes and to which everything returns.

As we bid farewell to our caves, leaving Neolithic times and moving into the Ancient World, we encounter the idea of *oikós*. The followers of the Greek philosopher Socrates (469–399 BCE) emphasised the equality of men and women and gave women responsibility and authority in the *oikós* (in running the household and managing the finances). Women were at the heart of providing food and tended the land to maintain material wealth.

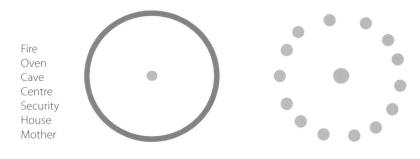

Fire
Oven
Cave
Centre
Security
House
Mother

Oikos (left) and *Ohana* (right) people are at the centre of their own lives, like the main character in a drama. *(fig. 7)*

But let's take another look at our cave, this time at the men. They sit round the fire and tell one another stories about the things they have experienced on hunting trips outside the cave. The male principle is generative and extroverted. Men are warriors and go out into the world – either with a sword or a ploughshare. It is mostly men who go to war. In a talk, the American corporate consultant Guy Kawasaki jokingly called the reason for this the 'killer gene'; according to Kawasaki, this gene makes men attack countries and build weapons, take over companies or bring them down.

Case study

Caroline lacks self-confidence. Having been given up for adoption as a baby by her alcoholic mother, she felt unloved. After later being abused by her adoptive father, she tried to find stability in a series of relationships, but she only found fulfilment at work.

The decision is made during therapy to separate the two subjects of abuse and adoption. Two family constellations are carried out with Caroline, in two sessions. The following healing sentences are spoken once the healing resolution formation for the adoption constellation has been found. The representative of the birth mother says: 'I am your mother and you are my daughter. I gave you away. I did this through love. I am sorry that I never saw you. I never saw myself. Please forgive me. Thank you.' Caroline then says: 'You are my mother and I am your daughter. Even though you gave me away, you will always be my mother. It is truly nothing but love. Thank you.'

Deep down, every adopted child is looking for its birth mother. However deep and painful the wounds may be, every person is striving to find that original safety and security – whether it's Caroline or Apple founder Steve Jobs (1955–2011). Every person is searching for this essence of life, and it's the same if you give a child away or take one on – it is truly only ever love that we are looking for and attempting to express.

Exercise

An exercise about healing sentences and healing rituals

Visualise your birth mother standing at a distance from you that is agreeable – that is, 'right' for you. Bow to her and say slowly: 'You gave birth to me. I spent nine months in your belly. My body comes from you. You brought me into the world, taking the risk of dying as you did so. You gave me life. Thank you.'

Now visualise your birth father standing at a distance from you that is agreeable – that is, 'right' for you. Bow to him and say slowly: 'You conceived me. Life came to me through you, and for that I thank you. Life is the most valuable thing and I shall make something of it. Thank you.'

What keeps a family together – some thoughts on the soul, the soul of a family and conscience

Family constellations aim to clear up two questions: (1) how are family relationships entangled and (2) what will untangle these relationships? Or, to put it the other way round: what connects the family, and how can shared love be ultimately victorious?

Here, we are talking about connective energies, in particular the soul, and the soul of families; the term 'soul' describes not only the spiritual essence of a person, as in Sanskrit (*ātman* = breath of life) or Hebrew (*rûah* = breath), but also a kind of psychological field that holds families together, so we also use words like loyalty and conscience. This is also why a constellation will touch upon psychological areas such as personality and motivations – that is, our reasons for doing things, sometimes against our better judgment.

In summary, we can say that in some respects a person will act according to individualist motivations, but in others is tied to the values of his or her family. We most often encounter this when people sabotage their own success as they unconsciously believe that they will be cast out from the tribe – the family – if they do better financially than their parents, for example. Many self-sabotage programmes have their roots in this loyalty to the family. For example, at a seminar held by the Swedish vision trainer Leo Angart, there was a woman who wore glasses out of unconscious loyalty to her mother even though she had good vision, and I met a woman at one of my own courses who, by her own admission, had got it into her head that she had diabetes in order to have something in common with her father and her brother.

This story is about a family's soul, values and behavioural patterns:

A tiger, a hunter and a bear

A hunter was once making his way through the thick undergrowth in the depths of the forest when he suddenly found himself face to face with a mighty tiger. Absolutely terrified, the hunter ran away and climbed the nearest tree, clambering higher and higher to escape the tiger's sharp claws. When he could climb no higher, he chanced upon a bear who had also escaped to the treetops. The tiger called to the bear, 'Hey, brother, look, here comes our common enemy. In his greed, he has killed countless animals and has decorated his halls with the heads and skins of your relatives. Human beings boast about being the acme of creation, but here is your opportunity: throw him down at my feet and he'll get what he's got coming to him.' The bear answered, 'Sir, this hunter has sought refuge in my house. It would not be right to hand over someone who seeks help. Indeed, even if this man has acted out of greed, it is beneath a creature of higher intelligence to hand over a weak and suffering creature to certain death.' Then the tiger said to the hunter, 'Hey, hunter, as you have heard, the bear won't do anything to you – throw him down here, go on, I am hungry and once I've eaten him, you can continue on your way unharmed. This is my promise to you on my honour as a tiger.'

The hunter gave the bear a hefty kick and knocked it off its branch. However, the bear quickly grabbed the next branch and managed to save itself. The tiger then spoke again, and with a voice like rolling thunder said, 'There, brother bear! There you see the contemptible attitudes of human beings. They look after only themselves. They cast aspersions on our Great Mother and their origins and they are the enemy of all living things. Now you know he wanted to kill you, you can hand him over without a second thought.' But the bear answered: 'I have never heard of revenge ever bringing benefit to any living being –

it's a poison that always kills those who dispense it. Paying back evil with evil is a great sin. I will never betray or give up the values of the bear, which are to meditate and search for truth; even if someone treats me maliciously, it is not right for me to demean myself through revenge.'

System error – exclusion and the problems it causes

A football team is famously made up of eleven players. If one is shown the red card and has to go and sit on the bench, the remaining ten players are affected as well; they somehow have to replace the one who's missing, finding a 'substitute' when they're not allowed to use an actual substitute. It's no different in a family: as soon as someone is removed from a family – because they don't fit into the family's image of itself, because they have gone away or because they have died* – someone else will have to represent them. The person who takes up this representative position is no longer in his or her own natural place and becomes, as it is known in systemic constellations, 'entangled' – but entangled in what? The person (and this can also be an object such as a house, for example) now has a different relationship to the family. Either consciously or unconsciously, this entangled person now tries to fulfil obligations, duties and expectations that are not at all their own and, as a result, displays behaviour that is not natural to their own being. The person is distanced further and further away from their own self. The conclusion: excluding a family member creates a problem and reincorporating the excluded person brings the solution.

---

* The term 'died' refers primarily to the victims of crimes of violence or casualties of war here.

Exercise

An exercise to make your life a success

For a few minutes every day from now on, find a quiet place where you can think about the following subjects:

Who am I?
What is my true place in life?
What are my goals?
What can I offer to life?

This daily meditation will lead you to the essence of life and to the only thing you can really call your own – yourself. Know yourself.

Whenever they had to answer big questions, the heroes of the Ancient World would go to the Temple of the Sun to seek the advice of the god Apollo so they could see clearly and lucidly. At the door of the shrine was the inscription 'Know thyself' (Greek: *gnothi seauton*), or in other words: 'Recognise yourself for who you are, and become the person that you are.' Healing means to become whole and/or complete, so we can only be happy when we feel complete – that is, when there is nothing in us that we reject.

You are the only person you may be with until the end of your life, and so it is of absolutely critical necessity that you love yourself, forgive yourself, are content with yourself and have found your centre.

Answer the following questions for yourself during your daily self-observation:

Is there someone in my family...
... with whose unhappy fate I identify?
... whose feelings I am helping to bear?
... whom I copy in order to atone for a sense of guilt?
... whom I copy to show up some unfairness?
... for whose fate I am trying to help take responsibility?
... (perhaps a deceased relative) whom I am trying to follow into death?

Environment

The American developmental biologist Dr Bruce Lipton carried out work at Stanford University back in the 1990s to prove that stem cells develop according to their environment. Whether a stem cell turns into connective tissue, a muscle or a nerve cell is dependent on its surroundings, and in the same way the development of a person is determined by their social and cultural milieu – by the language that is spoken, by the amount of love they receive and by the values, anxieties and cares that are part and parcel of life – and this influence begins with our prenatal experiences in the womb. Had you been born in another part of the world, you would now speak another language, have a different cultural background and, because of the values that had been passed on to you, you would think differently about yourself and the world around you. Indeed, had you grown up only a few hours away by plane, you might even hate the place where you now live – and that would be a pity, wouldn't it?

Motivated by a desire to complete the spiritual legacy of the German psychologist Martha Muchow (1892–1933), the Berlin university professor Kurt Lewin (1890–1947) carried out research on the influence of our environment. Having emigrated to the USA in 1933, he formulated the following theory there three years later: our behaviour (B) is dependent on our environment (E) and our personality (P). P and E are mutually dependent, leading Lewin to devise the following mathematical function: $B = f(E, P)$. We might thus ask ourselves the following question: 'Who am I, and who have I become under the influence of my psychological surroundings (which extend from the womb to my nursery and high school, and way beyond the street where I grew up)?' This is the same question asked by the eagle in the henhouse. Let's listen to his story.

The eagle in the henhouse

No one knows exactly how it happened – not even Henrietta, the wisest hen, can remember – but one morning, there lay among the eggs in the nest another egg that looked a bit different from the rest. 'Whatever,' she thought, and continued sitting on her clutch as usual. The chicks soon hatched, and one of them indeed looked a little bit different from the rest. It was also clumsier than the others, and as it wasn't as good at pecking up seeds, it was often teased. 'It's its own fault if it gets bullied,' said the hens – it didn't seem to want to fit in, after all. This hen didn't seem to like clucking or scratching and didn't get on with the nice cockerel. 'I want to fly properly, high in the sky, and hunt mice – that would be fun,' it said. 'Fun?' the others said to him contemptuously, 'that's just for idiots.' And so our hen sat down in a corner and dreamed of freedom while the pain he felt about his cramped quarters almost broke his heart. Of course, we know it wasn't a hen at all, but an eaglet.

One day, a dark shadow appeared on the ground. 'That's the shadow of the eagle,' they all cried, and then ran for their lives. The strange hen once again got the wrong end of the stick and didn't budge. 'The bird the others call the eagle must be that big strong hen,' it thought to itself. It gritted its beak and flapped onto a branch, using the technique it had been taught by the hens. As it sat there, the shadow appeared on the ground again and now – now our hen could see the eagle. It realised that it could no longer stay with the hens. It heard a voice deep within it saying: 'Follow the path of your destiny.' 'I am ready,' it said, then took to the skies like an eagle and was never seen again.

In 1956, the Canadian sociologist Erving Goffman (1922–1982) formulated a concept to describe roles that went on to become a psychological and scientific truism: every single person is permanently playing a role. Depending on the situation and surroundings in which we find ourselves at any given moment, we make use of a different aspect of our personality. Like actors in a play, we are able to slip into different roles on the stage of our lives; however, as all these roles are a part of our personalities, we remain ourselves even as we do this.

Exercise

An exercise to identify roles

Examine what effect various situations, people and places have on your behaviour. What roles do you play in your present family, in your birth family, at your workplace, at your social club, when you are at the counter in your bank or when you go to a garage, when you are sunbathing on the beach or eating in a restaurant? Also, examine what exactly is happening in your body and ask yourself which familial patterns and beliefs this might be connected with. What behavioural patterns have you adopted? Which decisions made in childhood have you never corrected, even though they have lost any validity or applicability? In a similarly critical way, ask yourself if you might possibly be copying a family member, if you identify with someone in your family or are trying to share some-one else's destiny. What debts might you possibly be wanting to settle? Here too, you can work with a table in your workbook. Divide the page into the following columns: (1) Surroundings, (2) Role, (3) Behaviour, (4) Feelings and emotions, (5) Destructive beliefs and (6) Copying and/or identification.

We have now found out about the power of the family constellation – and there's another method to come: the highly effective *ho'oponopono*, as used by the ancient Hawaiians. Both methods have the same aim in that they are intended to heal relationships and provide support for people in developing and unfolding their potential. I want to show you the potential that combining these two powerful methods can unlock – I bet you can't wait!

Hoʻoponopono

What is it?

Hoʻoponopono is one of the *kahuna* sciences, ancient shamanistic teachings from Hawaii, and describes a method for resolving personal problems and interpersonal conflict. The aim of *hoʻoponopono* is to heal relationships on many levels: (1) with yourself in particular, (2) with other people, (3) with your environment (nature) and (4) with the Source of all things.

Hoʻoponopono has been practised as a kind of family therapy and mediation for centuries, but over the last few decades it has developed from a traditional family conference into a self-help method that is nowadays often used in a simplified version. The heart of *hoʻoponopono* is a forgiveness ritual. By accepting, absolving, forgiving and reconciling, *hoʻoponopono* is an aid for life in three major areas of conflict: (1) relationships, partnerships and family, (2) profession, vocation and livelihood and (3) activating your powers of self-healing (by reducing stress, for example).

The meaning of the word

Depending on the context, *hoʻo* can mean 'to do, arrange or construct something'. Again depending on context, the word *pono* can be translated as (1) 'correct', (2) 'flexible' or even (3) 'compassion'. In relationships in particular, you have to be flexible and put your ego to one side. Overlooking little faults is not only compassionate but also makes life more pleasant, as it is generally true to say that people who make lots of rules in a relationship will live in close confinement, and who likes to live in a mental prison of their own devising? As the Hawaiian priest Haleaka Iolani Pule explained to me in 2012: 'With *ho'oponopono*, it's not about who's right or wrong, it's about good relationships.'

Putting things right again

Ho'oponopono can be translated literally as 'making things rightly right', 'putting things right again' or 'restoring divine order'. The idea behind it is that everything flows from the Source of all things (Hawaiian: *ke akua oi'a'io*), whose essence, *mana aloha*, is pure love. To the ancient Hawaiians, life was a great river (Hawaiian: *wai wai*) of material and spiritual wealth to which one needs only to turn and/or open up mentally and spiritually. Life itself is richness and a person living in harmony with him- or herself and the cosmos is able to live happily, healthily and in prosperity.

Re-establishing the cosmic order

The word *pono* appears twice, as two people are always required – both for a harmonious relationship in which all concerned can grow together, and for conflict, which can be exhausting. For a relationship to be fundamentally balanced, the solution to any problem has to be *pono* for all concerned: right for you and right for me. Right for people, right for animals, right for every plant and right for the Earth. The sole aim of this method of healing conflict at every level is to achieve a 'win-win' relationship – you are trying to create relationships in which everyone involved comes out on top. A 'win-lose' relationship – for example, in your professional life, when workers in third-world countries pay with their health because of precarious working conditions or when pesticides that harm the environment are used in agriculture – is really a 'lose-lose' relationship – everybody involved loses out, as you cannot base your happiness on the suffering of others.

Right – inside and out

Ponopono, 'right, inside and out', is based on the cosmic principle of resonances (Hawaiian: *kuolo*). This means, for example, that external environmental pollution will resonate within you in the form of a pollution of the heart. By the same token, considerate types of people who cause fewer problems for their fellow inhabitants on the planet would also suffer fewer lifestyle diseases themselves. But a hole in a heart with no love is a bottomless pit and will cry out to be filled. Symptoms of deficiency appear in the world only because of this vacuum in the heart, as the causal chain begins in the spirit. You could also say that everything is created twice – first in our imaginations and then on a material level.

Le 'ale'a ka 'ōlelo i ka pohu aku o loko.
If you are calm inside, everything
that leaves you is pleasant.

Hawaiian proverb

Right for you, right for me

When our thoughts and intentions are loving, compassionate and peaceful, the outcome will be a pleasant one. Just like everything else in the universe, *ponopono* obeys the fundamental law of cause and effect: *ka ua mea*. Everything we do and everything we fail to do has an effect. The circumstances of our lives are not there by coincidence, they are the result of our thoughts, the decisions we made on the strength of these thoughts and, ultimately, of our conscious and unconscious actions. It makes a difference whether you encourage or discourage a colleague with your remarks. It makes a difference whether you think well or badly of someone. It makes a difference whether you do sports or not, whether you are a good or a bad example to children, whether you shop sustainably or without thinking about the consequences. As an enfranchised being with the potential to create, we cast a vote for the world and for ourselves with everything we do. We shall harvest today what we sowed yesterday – and the same is true of tomorrow.

This law of cause and effect contains an incredible opportunity for humanity to heal Nature and bring about world peace; to stop being a 'spoilsport' in the ecosystem and return to being a team player in the great family of the world, we have to sow new causes – then we can reap a harvest of peace. Having peace in our hearts will lead to peace in the world.

The historic traditions of *ho'oponopono*

Shamanist *ho'oponopono*: healing the body

Ho'oponopono is the art of mediation and reconciliation, of settling, healing and resolving apparently hopeless situations. Whenever there was a problem in ancient Hawaii, a *kahuna-ho'oponopono* was called to heal it root and branch in the finest detail. This expert in *huna*, hidden knowledge, would investigate to see what spiritual causes had led to the conflict and once these had been corrected, order would return to the plane of material existence.

> The facilitator and mediator – *haku* and *tutu*
> The shaman – *kahuna-ho'oponopono*
> The companion of the gods – *kanaloa*

The facilitator in a family conference of this kind is known as the *haku* and is always to be seen as a natural authority. He (or she) acts as a neutral mediator between the conflicted parties – that is, between the victims, perpetrators and anyone else who has been embroiled in the drama (Hawaiian: *hihia*). Whenever there was a problem – either within the family or a personal issue such as an illness, for example – the *kahuna-ho'oponopono* was called. Much like the Greek therapist, this shaman was a servant of the gods who made his knowledge and experience available only to believers; one of the most important preconditions for the success of a *kahuna* in carrying out a *ho'oponopono* was trust. We know that faith can move mountains, and as soon as anyone displayed any doubts about the power of a *kahuna*, the shaman would recommend another expert, make his excuses and leave.

The classic image and role model of a great healer in the *huna* tradition is a kind of superman known as *kanaloa*. *Kane* translates as 'human' and 'spirit of god's spirit', and *loa* is the light from *mana loa*. *Kanaloa* was a companion of the gods who had amazing powers of healing thanks to the purity of his heart – a figure reminiscent of Jesus, who also had almost unlimited powers of healing.

Mai nana 'ino 'ino na hewa o kanaka
aka e huikala a ma 'ema 'e no.
Do not look upon the sins of a person with ill will –
instead, forgive and cleanse.

Queen Lili'uokalani (1838–1917)

Traditional *hoʻoponopono*: healing relationships

The first written records of *hoʻoponopono* are found in works published by the Hawaiian scientist and author Mary Kawena Pukui (1895–1986), who began to write about Hawaiian culture in the 1930s. These present *hoʻoponopono* to the West as a four-stage family therapy that attempts to cleanse misunderstanding and wrong behaviour by common accord. This could not have come at a better time, as American society was booming in the period after World War II and individualistic and client-centric psychotherapy, which drew heavily on the work of Sigmund Freud (1856–1939), was entirely accommodating to this new, system-orientated family therapy.

A summary of the four stages of a family conference*

In a traditional *hoʻoponopono*, the family would gather every evening in order to clear up anything that needed to be put to rest – possible misunderstandings, stress, relationship conflicts, differences of opinion, envy and anxieties – before sundown. No negative emotions or feelings were allowed to fester. This almost prophylactic ritual kept the family system stable as the following primary needs were met: acknowledgment, respect, integrity, loyalty.

(1) *pule*, connection: the family comes together to solve a problem (Hawaiian: *pilikia*). This is an inner gathering and a connection in prayer of all those present with the Source. Words are said aloud about the shared goals of the *ohana* and all present are blessed for success in what they are about to undertake.

---

* There is a complete overview of the stages of a family conference in the appendix.

(2) *mahiki*, examination of the problem: the participants discuss the subject in detail under the guidance of a facilitator, the *haku*, and accept personal responsibility. In order to improve mutual understanding here, the victim-perpetrator roles are swapped – each partner in conflict has to slip into the role of the other and speak and argue from this perspective.

(3) *mihi*, reparation and mutual forgiveness: anything material that is owed is returned. All participants ask for exoneration (on an intellectual level) and forgiveness (on an emotional level). All those involved forgive themselves unconditionally.

(4) *kala*, freedom through granting forgiveness: once all negative feelings have been released, all those involved signal their readiness to act constructively in a spirit of community from now on.

Similarities with the procedure for a family constellation will already be apparent here: the issue *(pilikia)*, the group *(ohana)*, the therapist *(haku)*, the representatives (swapping roles in the *mahiki*), moving towards a healing resolution (*mahiki* and *mihi*) and the healing resolution itself (reconciliation, *mihi* and *kala*).

Forgive before the sun goes down.

Hawaiian proverb

Modern *ho'oponopono*: helping you to help yourself

If you remember the television series *The Waltons*, you will be able to call to mind the image of an extended family (grandparents, parents and a host of children) that, every evening, would dutifully gather around the only radio (or later, the only television) in the house. This era came to an end in the 1970s – colour TV was introduced and more and more channels became available. Soon, every member of the family had their own TV set – and their own problems, too. Families broke apart to a certain extent, and help was required. For this reason, Morrnah Nalamaku Simeona, the great-niece of Mary Kawena Pukui (whom we met earlier), adapted the family conference for modern conditions by integrating Christian and Indian elements and reconfiguring it as a method of helping people to help themselves. It now became possible to practise *ho'oponopono* alone, without a *haku* as a facilitator between the warring parties. This method follows twelve steps, including prayers.

Simplified *ho'oponopono*: a formula for peace in four sentences

The four-stage *ho'oponopono* has become better known over the last few years. This version stems from Dr Ihaleakala Hew Len, a pupil of Morrnah Nalamaku Simeona, who made a name for himself in the 1980s by healing several mentally ill convicted criminals with his simplified form of the *ho'oponopono*.* The aim of this simplified *ho'oponopono* is to resolve conflict quickly and to regain inner equilibrium – that is, as an individual, to move away from separation towards the centre, and thus towards healing. In the centre you will

---

* You can find out more about this in Ulrich Emil Duprée: *Ho'oponopono. The Hawaiian forgiveness ritual as the key to your life's fulfillment*. Earthdancer 2012.

find a way to expunge the dysfunctional memories – you might also call these neural data – that make a problem into more than it actually is. Conflicts often arise that are only tangentially connected with the issue and whose roots are in our perceptions and in the trauma and memories of our early childhoods.

> I'm sorry. Please forgive me. I love you. Thank you.

These four sentences and/or stages in the modern *ho'oponopono* are a summary of the middle section of the traditional *ho'oponopono* – mutual forgiveness (Hawaiian: *mihi*) – and it is the simplicity of this peace formula in particular that is a distinguishing feature of the whole *ho'oponopono* concept of conflict.

I'm sorry.

I accept the negative things and/or the things within me that stand in the way of love. I'm sorry that I and my ancestors have harmed you and your ancestors, either consciously or unconsciously. I'm sorry that I have harmed others and disturbed their development, either consciously or unconsciously. I regret this and I apologise.

Please forgive me. – I forgive myself.

I forgive myself for the negative things within me. I forgive myself for putting myself in that position. I forgive myself for being a perpetrator. I ask to be forgiven for being part of the problem. I forgive myself because I feel guilty. I forgive the perpetrator and let go of him and of my victimhood.

I love myself. – I love you.

I respect myself and I respect you. I love myself with all my weaknesses and I accept myself for what I am. I love what exists. I have faith that this situation will help me progress. I respect the situation that is showing me what to do. I love the situation that has come to me to bring me back into the flow of life. I see the divine in you and I see the divine in me. I will use this realisation and reshape the situation. Love is the only power and the greatest power in the universe.

Thank you.

I thank you for the blessing hidden within this situation. I thank you for this transformation. I thank you for this realisation. Thank you for the experience I have had. Thank you for the best solution for me and for all those involved. I allow this healing. I thank you for this miracle. I thank you for my life.

With the words 'thank you', you are giving permission for healing and for 'deleting the data', as it were, that led to the conflict. You say thank you when you receive something and, as you can't think of two things at the same time, you immediately go from having a deficit of gratitude to an abundance. Saying thank you means believing and/ or being convinced that you have already received something – it would be crazy to say thank you while standing there empty-handed. You can't fool the universe by simply having the intention to receive and saying thank you in advance. Inner doubt is the original impulse (Sanskrit: *vrit*) and it is highly effective. In addition to doubt, fear and lack of trust, a further obstacle to healing and/or cleansing is that lots of people would love to be healthy but are not prepared to do anything about it. The main reason for this is that there is another 'hidden pay-off': they unconsciously believe that a need (for example, for acknowledgment or peace) is being met by maintaining the problem

Connecting and releasing – family constellations and *ho'oponopono*

Peace begins with me

The Hawaiian author Mary Kawena Pukui, whom we met earlier, says a successful *ho'oponopono* has two ingredients: honesty and responsibility. The Hawaiian forgiveness ritual investigates a person's 'share' in a problem. If there is someone in your family who is excluded, addicted to drugs or chronically ill, for example, you can ask what you have done or not done for that person to end up in such a situation. Ask yourself, 'What did I do to make … (include here the name of the person in question and their relationship to you) choose this path?' – always remembering that you are not guilty, you are just involved. When you now stand opposite this relative in a family constellation (either with a group or alone with floor anchors), you can say, for example, 'I'm sorry that I did… (outline your 'share'). Please forgive me. I forgive myself for my destructive actions now. I love you. Thank you for this healing.'

In a traditional *ho'oponopono*, both the family of the victim and the family of the perpetrator would gather and people would question themselves on how the particular events could have come about, asking: 'What did I do and/or not do to make X a perpetrator? What did I do and/or not do to make Y a victim?' The roles would then be swapped – that is, the family of the victim would take the role of the family of the perpetrator and vice versa. The actual questions that all those involved would ask were: 'If I were to behave like X (the perpetrator), why would I be doing that? What programmes are there within me that led me to be confronted with this issue?'

As we are often blind to our own behaviour and actions, a *ho'oponopono* can bring us valuable insights; the swapping of roles between perpetrator and victim in mediation processes or attempts at conciliation in wage negotiations are good examples of this. In our case, systemic constellations combined with *ho'oponopono* can be extremely helpful in achieving an optimal outcome for all concerned and creating synergies from the understanding achieved.

Huna and the shamanist teachings of Hawaii

Ho'oponopono is part of *huna*, the ancient shamanist teachings of Hawaii. Just as the British lumped together the various philosophical and religious traditions beyond the Indus under the term 'Hinduism', the American linguist Max Freedom Long (1890–1971) grouped together the extensive system of wisdom and teachings used by the ancient Hawaiians under the heading *huna*. *Huna* means knowledge and wisdom. If you want to build up a business, for example, theoretical knowledge is not enough; you also have to make use of your experience – your wisdom – to take decisive action and use *ho'oponopono* to build up good client relationships. If you are bringing up children, it helps to find out about the development of a child's mind from books written by experts, so you can act wisely and prudently. *Huna* can thus be applied in very practical circumstances to our own time. In this system practised by *kahunas*, experts in *huna*, there are seven precepts that you will be able to integrate into family constellations, with appropriate exercises. These seven concepts for inner and outer harmony are called *ike* (perception), *kala* (freedom), *makia* (focus), *mana* (energy), *manawa* (the moment), *aloha* (love) and *pono* (flexibility).

Ike – perspective: the world is subjective

The way that all human beings have their own personal view of themselves and of the world is known in *huna* as *ike*. This notion includes such things as a person's individual point of view, their physical and mental state, social and cultural background, education and intentions.

Every kind of observation is always subjective. One of the decisive insights achieved by quantum physics is to realise that the consciousness (Hawaiian *noo noo*) of the observer exerts an influence on a quantum cloud* of probabilities and creates reality by observing it. The opinions that people form about themselves and about the world become reality. *Ike* means that you are what you think about yourself. Are you an independent thinker? Do you take time to look at a topic, or do you let others form your opinion?

Getting worked up about the world is pointless.
The world won't be impressed.

Marcus Aurelius (121–180 CE)

---

* In quantum physics, the smallest building blocks of material and energy are known as quanta. If you try to observe these quanta, you see that they are no longer tied to a clearly defined position and seem to dissolve into a kind of cloud. This creates an infinite number of possibilities for where something might be located or occur.

Exercise

An exercise with floor anchors

On the floor anchors, write the words (1) Me, (2) Family, (3) World and (4) Neutral observer. Arrange these in a way that makes sense for them and try to get a feeling for each of the four terms (subsystems) in turn. What image do you have of yourself? What do you think of yourself and your family? Is your family a place of security and safety or do you find family celebrations threatening? How do you view the world? How are you perceived by the world and by your family? Do you belong to your family or do you feel unappreciated? How does the neutral observer see the situation? Examine your relationships and the images you have formed of yourself and your environment, write these down in your workbook and add the date. Repeating the exercise at intervals (about every three months) will help you track your progress. (Floor anchors, see p. 45.)

Every person has an opinion: the nature that a person ascribes to the world on the basis of their memories (their mental data) is the way it will seem to them. This way of seeming is their reality, and only the sum of all realities can make up real reality (Ancient Egyptian: *Re Al* = pervaded by cosmic consciousness). A conscious attempt to understand the behaviour of other people is the first step towards healing and reconciliation. Understanding yourself and the world is the declared path and ultimate goal of all philosophers, mystics and scientists. Indeed, even in the world of diplomacy, people try to understand one another in order to maintain good relations. Having good relationships means understanding one another, and this can only be achieved by talking to one another.

Exercise

An exercise on the topic of rejection

Visualise a person whom you reject because of their views. Imagine this person standing before you at a distance you are comfortable with. Mentally bow and say: 'I'm sorry that I have judged you because of your opinions. Please forgive me. I forgive myself for that now. I respect you and thank you for this realisation. I thank you for healing all those involved.'

Possible healing sentences in a simplified ho'oponopono with a family constellation: I'm sorry that I have never tried to understand your point of view before. I am here and you are there. Please forgive me. I forgive myself. Thank you for this realisation and thank you for healing all those involved.

Makia – focus: energy follows attention

Makia describes the psychological phenomenon whereby things in our world become more important as soon as we direct our attention towards them. You will no doubt have had the feeling at some point or another in your life that a person's behaviour left something to be desired. Let's say someone you live with (your partner or your roommate, for example) doesn't take the rubbish out. Over time, it begins to irk you more and more; you can't think of anything else, you start to waste your energy on it – and instead of talking about it, you react either by attacking or retreating. However, you can use this mental principle to guide your life in any direction you want: if you want to improve your relationships with others, concentrate on what you can admire and praise. Give an answer rather than always reacting on the principle of 'fight or flight'. It has been psychologically proven, by the way, that people behave according to our expectations. An American teacher once told me about some experiments in which teachers were warned about certain students. Although these students had got good grades in the preceding year, they went on to do less well in these teachers' assessments. Now examine how your opinions about people in your day-to-day life change and how you are almost predefined by the statements made about you and the prejudices and expectations placed upon you by others.

Possible healing sentences in a simplified ho'oponopono with a family constellation: I'm sorry. I forgive myself for my prejudice. I forgive you for your prejudice. I love you. Thank you. I'm sorry that I have pressurised others with my expectations. Please forgive me. I love you. Thank you. I'm sorry that I have tried to manipulate you. Please forgive me. I forgive all the people who have tried to manipulate me. I love you. Thank you.

Life gets more pleasant when you contemplate what you have rather than complaining about what you don't have.

Marcus Aurelius (121–180 CE)

Kala – freedom: there are no boundaries, only opportunities

Freedom through forgiveness
Freedom of thought
Freedom through actions

It is a fundamental principle that you have the freedom to shape your life as you wish. If you happen to bear a grudge against your parents, for example, for something that happened 20, 30 or 40 years ago, I would like to ask you to take your foot off these mental and emotional brakes. Only you can do this – who else did you think would do it? Forgiveness does not undo what was done, but it frees you from mental and physical toxins that prematurely age cells. Those whose tunnel vision means that they are only able to dwell on past events with anger or resentment miss out on the beauty that is everywhere around them.

The sun isn't always shining, of course, but you can tell how mature someone is by how long they stay furious. People who can't let go are pretty much just 'treading water'. They are stuck in their past and fear the future – and because they can't let go of their resentment, they often do damage to themselves and to others. Successful people, however, forgive quickly, concentrate on the solution and are more interested in the future.

The sum total of all the circumstances of our lives is the outcome of our thoughts. We think, make decisions and act. Everything we do or don't do bears fruit in our lives. We have the freedom to do sport or not. We have the freedom to stand by and watch bees die out or not. If we don't look after our health, we get sick and if we take our relationships with our partners for granted, they will suffer. How often we would like to change something in our network of relationships but don't have the courage, the decisiveness, the perseverance and the strength of will (Hawaiian: *mana mana*). Those are the times we are lacking energy, lacking *mana*.

Possible healing sentences in a simplified ho'oponopono with a family constellation: I'm sorry that I have held you back for so long. Please forgive me. I forgive myself that I have blocked myself for so long. I am letting go and I thank you for the best solution for us. Thank you for this healing.

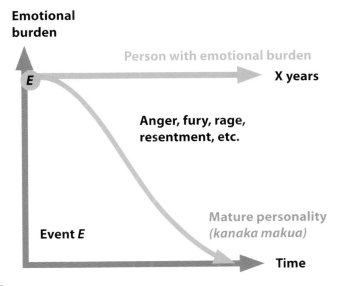

fig. 9

Mana – energy: one for all and all for one

Like every Hawaiian word, *mana* also has several definitions. Depending on the context, it can mean 'energy', 'ability', 'personal strength' or 'strong personality'. The idea behind *mana* is that we become aware of the spiritual power within us and that this is exhibited by us as strength, ability and authority. This source (Hawaiian: *kumu*) of power is revealed in your talents and in your wisdom. *Mana* means energy, and when you fully embody your gifts, maintain good relationships, stand up for yourself and accept your family as it is, you will have energy. *Mana* can be generated, transmitted, bequeathed and also recovered.

Turn your face to the sun and the shadows will fall behind you.

African proverb

Exercise

*An exercise in acknowledging your parents
and thereby attaining your own strength*

In your workbook, make a list of all your abilities, talents and gifts. Write down everything you are good at doing and everything you like doing. Think about yourself – get your workbook out in the morning at breakfast and add to your list of praiseworthy qualities, even noting such banal things as 'I make a really great cup of tea'. This will help you enormously in developing positive energy.

Now write a list with all your parents' abilities, talents and gifts. This might be a bit of a challenge. If you come to very destructive behaviour on the part of one of your parents, deliberately ignore it and look for some light in the darkness. Good relationships and happiness don't come about by chance – they are the result of conscious efforts. People who put an effort into *ho'oponopono* are like prospectors for gold; you find gold in mud, in earth and in the ground, but you dig for gold – and not to find dirt.

Manawa – the time is right: full steam ahead

If you ask people when is the right moment to act – for example, to make an important telephone call, to ask someone for forgiveness, to give up a bad habit or to make a decisive life change – almost everyone will answer (with a smile), 'Now – now is the best time.' But if you ask the same people the next day whether they have started, almost all of them will shake their head. I too have had to learn from bitter experience that 'today' is not in fact the best moment to do something important – yesterday was. Well, fine, so yesterday was the best moment, but today is still an option, as today is tomorrow's yesterday. The only moment of strength is 'now' – and this is what *manawa* means. You can only act in the now, and that moment of now is always, as there is no other point in time that you can actively experience: the past has gone and the future will always be a step ahead of you – time flows towards it like a river. In the next exercise, we will go for a bit of a swim, removing dangerous stones from the flow of time (Hawaiian: *ala nou ana*) and so changing the present and the future for the better.

An exercise about the flow of time

On separate pieces of paper, write the words (1) Past, (2) Present and (3) Future. Arrange these floor anchors in the room in a formation that makes emotional sense to you. Once again, jot down everything that occurs to you during this exercise in your workbook, as these details will be extremely useful for your future path. (Floor anchors, see p. 45.)

Stand on the paper marked 'Present', the now, and let your feelings flow into the moment. What does this point in time hold? Use the helpful list in the appendix to describe what you are feeling. Now look back at the past. What are you feeling? What are you experiencing as you examine your past? Next look to your future and ask yourself what reaction that evokes in you. Having done this, go and stand first on the 'past' paper and then the 'future' and look in the various directions from each. Give yourself time and be conscious of all the feelings that arise in you. How does your future feel when you are aware that from there, you can only look back? What feelings does that elicit? How do you feel when you can only look forward from the past? What is the past trying to say to the present and the future? What would the future like to say to the past and the present? What is the child saying to the adult, and what are you as a physically aged person saying to the younger you right now? What can you see?

Go and stand on the 'Present' again and realise that you can look in both directions from here. What would you like to say to the past now, and what to the future? Use the four sentences from the simplified *ho'oponopono* as healing sentences here: 'I'm sorry. Please forgive me. I love you. Thank you.' If it feels right for you, add: 'I bless you with all my heart.'

Life gives us the things we concentrate on and we have the relationships we permit ourselves. These are the spiritual principles of *ike, makia, kala* and *mana*. If we only ever do and think what we have always done and thought, we will only continue to receive what we have always received in the past; to change this, we have to think and act differently. We are sowing new causes. I have the following power question for you, which I would love you to answer – you can take a few days to do it if you like: if you feel guilty about something or regret something, and you were to repeat this exercise in a year – what would you have to do to know that you have done your best not to have to feel guilty or regret something or feel sorry for yourself? Little by little, bring about a healing resolution in your life in which the present releases itself from the painful experiences of the past. Once the past has asked for forgiveness and the present has granted this, ask the present for forgiveness too – for example: 'I'm sorry that I held on to you for so long. I'm sorry that I only saw your negative aspects. I'm sorry that I was unable to see the gifts you gave. Please forgive me. I love you. Thank you.'

In the present, ask for the blessing of the future *(kūkulu kumuhana)*. Also, ask the future directly what you can do in the present to bring about a solution. To do this, go back and stand in the 'future' position. The healing resolution will ultimately be a free and reinforced view from the 'present' in all directions.

Aloha – love: being happy with what is

There is a rule in *huna* that is fundamental to all else, and it goes like this: 'Never harm, always help.' This is the *aloha* philosophy that recognises the divine in every living creature, whether human, animal or plant. It is the foundation of all yoga practice and the essence of all religions. Everything comes from the Source and denying the divine presence in a living creature would mean rejecting the divinity itself. This is what Jesus meant when he said you should hate the sin but love the sinner. Nowadays, however, we tend to do it the other way round – we hate people because they insult us, get in our way or aren't nice to us. But allow me one question: might it be possible that we are behaving equally as badly, or even worse, when we exploit the Earth, drive out its aboriginal inhabitants and treat their traditions as beneath us, and justify the death of animals for the maintenance of our standards of living?

The Source, the rain, the sun and love have no ego-driven intentions. The Source does not judge, it shares its love *(mana aloha)* with everyone. Recognising the spiritual origins of all living creatures – and therefore the equality and unity of all these living creatures – is the route to knowledge, wisdom and a special kind of humility. Humility does not mean being subservient, it means not placing yourself arrogantly above others. It prevents people from becoming envious or covetous, and from judging their peers.

Alo means 'being together', 'sharing something with one another' and 'spiritual essence'. *O* is 'the whole', and this is the *O* in the great *ohana*. *Oha* means 'joy and affection' and *ha* is 'breath'. *Aloha* means (1) sharing the same spiritual essence with all living creatures, (2) recognising your own origins in the divine, spiritual essence and (3) feeling and acting in connection with all other living beings, with divine creation and with your divine origins (Hawaiian: *ke akua oi'a'io*). This love shows itself in your level of contentment with life in the here and now – that is, being happy with things as they are – and in doing what needs to be done.

Pono – flexibility: effectiveness is the yardstick of truth

There is no magic bullet for everyone, and the methods available are as different as we are – allopathy, traditional Chinese medicine, Ayurveda and homeopathy are just some examples. There are more than a hundred different kinds of therapy that specialise in spiritual matters, so there is something for everyone. Whatever helps in the moment is right. You have to be flexible and (1) take advice from a range of responsible experts before ultimately (2) making a confident choice. Those who are unable to make a choice should not be surprised if others do it for them, however.

The aim of a relationship could be said to be both that each person has their own needs satisfied and that all involved satisfy each other's needs while simultaneously serving the greater good of the whole. This is known as 'living in a co-committed relationship'. In a co-committed relationship, everyone involved in the system wins, whereas in a co-dependent relationship, every participant loses.* With co-dependence, each partner has unconsciously made an invisible contract to tolerate the bad habits of the other; here, each only seems to derive benefit from not having to change – not changing means not growing.

---

* See 'win-win relationship' and/or 'win-lose relationship' on p. 72.

Pono, flexibility, seems to apply to people with strong characters in particular, as weaker personalities are driven by their destructive habits – for example, the tendancy to complain, to succumb to rage, to take offence, to emotionally blackmail or punish others, or an inability to give in. By contrast, people with strong characters look to the well-being of others and try to find common ground. *Pono* also means offering no further resistance to the opinions *(ike)* of others and accepting and acknowledging them. If you have ever tried to change your partner, you will know the hopelessness of this undertaking, and this is why wise people choose to be a silent role model, humbly moving towards the ideal of what they would like to be – you're trying to make up the ground between what you are and what you could be.

Case study

Lizzie, 42 with no children, is married to an alcoholic. She is begin-ning to wonder how long she can maintain her hopes and cling to the illusion that her partner will one day stop drinking. She was beaten as a child by her alcoholic father and so cannot understand why she is still persisting with the marriage. What benefit is she deriving from this situation? She has asked for advice.

We begin with a ho'oponopono session. We sit in a circle with Lizzie and about 20 other people and search the group's 'shares' with our hearts in order to find clarity. Having attuned as a group to the mood of the meeting (pule), we investigate the problem (mahiki) by getting all those involved to search for their share (hihia) in the problem. We then immediately resolve these shares with mutual forgiveness (mihi) and so release the negative potential (kala) in its entirety.

The following questions are asked in the circle:

(1) 'If I were to behave like Lizzie, why would I do that?' NB: The task is not to analyse Lizzie and look for her motivation, as people are so keen to do in order to justify their own shortcomings. No, the task is to look for the shadows in your own life: 'Are there areas in my life where I behave in a similar manner? What do I cling to even though it harms me? Where do I make compromises that damage me? What am I afraid of? What doubts prevent me from following my path?'

(2) 'What has caused this topic to come specifically to me?' In other words: 'Why has the topic of alcoholism and the inability to break free come to me as a seminar participant? Is there a direct message in Lizzie's topic for me?'

Exercise

A little exercise

Provide at least three answers to each of the two questions posed above. Note these in your workbook and then say to yourself as you look at your answers: 'I'm sorry. Please forgive me. I forgive myself now. I love myself, and I love you. Thank you for this healing.'

Ohana – the outer family

Just like every Hawaiian word, *ohana* has numerous meanings related to Nature, and these reflect the unity of the whole and the oneness of Nature. *Ohana* means, for example, 'several plants with a common root'. *Ohana* is a tribe or clan whose members all have their roots in common forebears, their ancestors. Although the term used to be applied strictly to refer to the family, nowadays an organisation or a company is considered an *ohana*. These are kinds of tribes that set themselves apart from others through their common goals, language (for example, professional jargon, youth slang, dialects), clothing (for example, a uniform, business suit or special sports clothing) and behaviour.

O is the symbol for the whole, for the Earth, for connectedness and for the Source. *Hana* means 'deed', 'work', 'task'. *Ha* is outflowing breath. *Na* is a suffix used to create nouns. The members of an *ohana* are therefore people who (1) sit in a circle and (2) breathe together, who (3) share a common task for the good of the whole and (4) are connected with the Source. An *ohana* is typically a system in which every member is involved in communal life, such as in education, for example, or in earning a living.

How a forest survives the ages

The trees in Redwood Forest, a national park in California, grow very tall. Majestic and powerful, they have stood for decades, even centuries, and between them have experienced endless storms and hurricanes. Indeed, these trees have survived mighty snowstorms and devastating earthquakes – even though their roots only go down a few metres. What is their secret? Where does their special power to survive even earthquakes unscathed lie? According to the park rangers, the reason for their communal survival is their 'connectedness' – their almost infinite network of roots. Underground, well out of sight of those who stroll through the forest, each tree is interwoven with its fellows. Whether giant tree or new growth, each one is held in place by its surroundings. Almost as a gesture of love, the older trees offer the younger ones the embrace of their roots and the saplings gratefully receive these and intertwine with them. Every tree, both great and small, is connected to and rooted in the entire forest.

A*umakua* – the ancestors

No one is alone in the *ohana* – you are connected horizontally with all the living members and vertically with a chain of ancestors reaching far back into the past. Each member of the *ohana* feels connected to the Source through his or her ancestors – and the term for this is *aumakua*, which means both 'tribal god' and 'ancestor'. The same is also true of a family constellation: the client in a constellation is not an isolated being – by sitting in front of the group and beside the therapist, you are, as it were, sitting down in your imagination with your parents and ancestors.

Exercise

An exercise about the origins of
the chain of ancestors

Sit down, relax and breathe easily before asking yourself how far back
your chain of male and female ancestors reaches. Where did you begin?
Meditate on this and go a long way back in your thoughts. Be clear in
your mind that your chain of ancestors stretches right back to the Source.
A connection of this kind through space and time gives strength and
stability. If you have a bone to pick with your parents, look further and
further back. Feel the power that flows to you from your cosmic parents
as soon as you open yourself up to it. Meditate about this connectedness
with your ancestors, who bring you blessings.

Healing your relationship with your parents
through forgiveness

Therapists throughout the world can sum up the topic from which
95 per cent of their clients suffer in just two words: 'the parents'.
A few things have certainly gone wrong in the generations that
precede us, but this only has the importance that we allow it *(ike,
makia, kala, pono)*. If someone is carrying great hurt within them, it
is likely that this hurt will be paid forward – and this has to be
forgiven. If a classic family constellation has given rise to concern
about this in the past, the children can indeed give their parents, and
the parents their children, free and heartfelt forgiveness in a
ho'oponopono; no one takes a superior position over the other in such
circumstances, nor is anyone humiliated. There is no manipulation,

as all base reasons for action are alien to the Hawaiian forgiveness ritual. You forgive because you wish to find peace and a new and unburdened beginning. The pain may sometimes sit deep, but you can still take small steps and say: 'I open myself to the possibility of forgiving you.'

Stanford University is renowned for its research in the field of behavioural psychology and the following experiment provides much food for thought:

The five monkeys

In the first part, five monkeys are let into an experimental area, about 20m² in size, where there is a ladder allowing access to a few tasty bananas. As soon as one of the monkeys climbs the ladder to fetch the fruit, however, the behavioural researchers spray the four monkeys standing below with water from a garden hose. This procedure is repeated several times with the same monkeys – every time one of the five monkeys tries to fetch the bananas for himself, the others are soaked. At some point the monkeys will have had enough, and as soon as one of the *ohana* tries to clamber up the (career) ladder, he is hauled down by the others and beaten up.

In the second part of the experiment, one of the five monkeys is substituted. The new monkey sees and smells the bananas immediately, of course, but as soon as this unsuspecting wretch climbs the ladder, he is dragged down and beaten by the others as they are scared of being soaked. 'Huzzah,' think these four, 'we're staying dry', while the horrified fifth monkey is thinking: 'What is up with these crazy monkeys?' A second monkey is now substituted, and the new arrival also wishes to climb the ladder. He is quickly pulled down by the others – and now the first substitute monkey cheerfully joins in with the beating. The second monkey probably asks the others what on earth is going on in this *ohana*, only to be told: 'Bananas get you soaked.' Each monkey is in turn swapped out for another one, such that after a while, there are no monkeys left who have ever been soaked, but each new monkey is beaten up as soon as he tries to get at the bananas. None of the monkeys knows why it is dangerous or forbidden to fetch the bananas – but that is the programming from the 'ancestors'. And don't we humans behave in a similar way when we take precepts like 'money spoils your character' on board during childhood, and still follow them, even though we have never tested their truthfulness as an adult?

Ancestral programming as a download

We inherit our ancestral programming in the same manner as we download programs (in the truest sense of the word) on to a data carrier.* The stem cell researcher and developmental biologist Dr Bruce Lipton, whom we met earlier, assumes that we are already taking on these programs as prenatal experiences during the embryo stage, and we soak them up like a sponge into our childhood years. The reason for this is that brainwaves in childhood are located in particular in the slow theta range, allowing us not only to learn several languages at once but also to quickly comprehend how to behave within our clan and how to think of others. If you had grown up in a family of Masai, you would have absorbed ancestral programming with your mother's milk that was entirely different from that usually found in a Western European family.

Take a look at your own life: what did you hear and/or perceive in your childhood? How did people talk about your neighbours, about

---

* See '*Unihipili* – The lower self, subconscious and inner child', p. 121.

money, about themselves, in your vicinity? What effect did all these commonplaces have on your life? Do you have similar physical complaints to one of your parents? What habits do you have? Are you more like your father or your mother than you would like – and why don't you like it?

To be free, it helps to get to grips with the events and the legacy of your past. Think of the way destructive ancestral programming, patterns and convictions are passed on, like pails of water in a 'bucket brigade' – and it is up to you what you make of this. In a ritual in a classic family constellation, you might possibly hand back this water pail (to stay with the image), saying: 'I honour your destiny, but this does not belong to me. Please look kindly upon me if I give it back to you.' In a *hoʻoponopono* combined with a family constellation, you are opening a door by accepting this pail of water. You accept and honour what you have received from your ancestors and consider in the here and now how you can transform this to your advantage. You ask for the gift in a *hoʻoponopono* – what blessings might be hidden away? Instead of giving the pail of water back, you can pour the water on your plants and use the pail as a plantpot later. Many people later use precisely what they have experienced in childhood to help others in similar situations. It is up to you and your imagination what you make of the gifts of life.

Case study

Angie's father was given to fits of rage and she had adopted this behaviour from him. She had given the anger back in a family constellation, but nothing changed.

In a ho'oponopono, Angie realises that lying hidden in her father's anger are both enormous power and a gift. Rage is the absence of love. This explosive form of anger is on the dark side, as it were; rage is the shadow side, turned away from love, with the characteristics that allow you to distance yourself, to give your opinion, to stand up for yourself or assert yourself – positive characteristics that anyone would surely wish for themselves, but Angie had inherited none of these positive traits (mana).* Instead, Angie only got loud, like her father, harming herself and others.

During an ancestral constellation with ho'oponopono, Angie accepts the hidden gift from her father – inner strength and a healthy ability to assert herself – and from now on will focus only on this light side. The healing sentences she speaks aloud after bowing to the representative of her father are: 'My dear father, I'm sorry that I rejected you. It was your anger that hurt me. I realise that you and your anger are two different things. Please forgive me. I accept you now and take on your strength, your self-assertion, your ability to distance yourself and to stand up for yourself. I am stepping out of the shadow into the light. I love you and thank you with all my heart for this legacy. Thank you for this healing of all those involved in the here and now.'

From now on, Angie will consciously no longer pay heed to the shadow of 'rage'. She now owns her own strength and can self-

---

* There is more about this in the chapter 'The parents, the elders, the wise and the teachers', p. 118.

confidently follow her own path. She radiates authority without having to be authoritarian.

Accepting your parents and being accepted by them

Would you like to be accepted by your parents just as you are? Of course you would! So what do you think of a win-win solution in which you accept your parents just as they are? This is likely to be a real challenge for many people, but as we have already learned: energy flows to where your attention is *(makia)*. We can only receive what we ourselves are prepared to give.

Possible healing sentences for a simplified ho'oponopono with a family constellation: I'm sorry that I couldn't accept you as you are. I'm sorry that I nonetheless expected you to accept me as I am. I'm sorry I was so angry at you. I'm sorry I was so angry at myself. I'm sorry that I rejected myself. Please forgive me. I forgive myself now. I accept you just as you are. I love you and I love myself. I accept myself just as I am – with all my weaknesses and all my strengths. Thank you for this realisation. Thank you for this healing of all involved.

A family conference about birth

A family constellation drills down to the absolute essentials, such as your father, your mother and your relationship with them. Birth and death are also essential elements of this – they are both gateways into realms that we are unable to revisit when we like. There is the realm of the living and the realm of those who have gone before. We are here and they are there. At the same time, souls continually decide to visit this world and as a result birth was a special event for the ancient Hawaiians: someone had chosen to appear in the *ohana*, and his or her arrival was anticipated with joy and mindfulness. It is said that Hawaiian women never used to suffer from pain in childbirth; why should Mother Nature cause women pain as they brought a child into the world? This was an absurd notion for the ancient Hawaiians. Mary Kawena Pukui described a case in which a woman felt great pain as her contractions began; the only possible reason for this was that there was still unfinished business *(hala)* between the family members – something had not been cleansed. This was why this soul (Hawaiian: *kane* = spirit of god's spirit) did not wish to make an appearance in their family. A *ho'oponopono* was called at once and a *ho'omala*, a purification ceremony, was performed. As not every member of the family could be present, stones were set up as representatives. Once all the reservations between the family members and the representatives had been cleared out of the way, the birth went without a hitch. Here too, the combination of *ho'oponopono* and a family constellation led to healing.

Exercise

An exercise in resolving subjects in which other people are also burdened (hihia)

Lay out four floor anchors: (1) one for you, (2) one for a family member that you have not yet forgiven for something and remain at odds with, (3) one for the *hihia* – that is, a person who has been caught up in events (in the case study on page 116, this was an unborn child) and (4) one for the neutral observer. Stand on each of the floor anchors in turn, and search your emotions. What are you feeling? What is your partner in the conflict feeling? How does the person who has been caught up in the situation feel? How does the neutral observer feel? Standing in your own position, speak a forgiveness ritual *(mihi)* in all directions: 'I'm sorry that … (say what you are sorry about here). Please forgive me. I love you. Thank you.' Now move to the position of the person with whom you were at odds. How has their position changed? Now point the forgiveness ritual in the opposite direction and have that person perform the ceremony. Now rearrange the floor anchors so that the situation is getting closer to a win-win solution and feels good for all concerned. Always search your feelings as you stand in each position. Repeat this mutual forgiveness until you are able to identify a healing resolution in which you feel released from all those negative memories. (Floor anchors, see p. 45.)

The parents, the elders, the wise and the teachers

Anyone obliged to hike through deep snow, in Alaska or Siberia or similar places, would be wise to follow in the footsteps of those who have gone before; on your own and following your own path, you would soon be stuck in deep snowdrifts. In the same way, intelligent people walk in the footsteps of their teachers and follow the trails they have blazed. People who would like to be successful are best advised to do the same – that is, do what other successful individuals before them have done. If you want to be an outstanding chef, you have to learn your trade from the best cooks, and if you want to be a good singer, you have to take lessons from successful vocalists. In the West, however, we have the unappealing habit of learning from others but subsequently, at some point or another, criticising our teachers. We have learned as pupils and then what we give back is not gratitude but ridicule for their many weaknesses. In the Eastern tradition, it is considered stupidity or a *faux pas* to insult your parents, elders, ancestors or your teacher, as in so doing you rob yourself of all the positive outcomes of their good deeds. In ancient traditions, people would walk in the footsteps of their teacher and only follow their own path when they reached the end of these tracks. Having reached such a point, you ask for a blessing and with these good wishes, you join the unbroken chain of the teachers who have preceded you (a chain just like that of your ancestors) and take their great achievements still further. So, in the Eastern tradition, you always show gratitude and respect, despite any differences of opinion you may have, as you realise that you have not had to find out anything for yourself up to this point on your path; you have received all your knowledge through the charity and goodwill of your teacher.

The blessings and abilities that a master, teacher, elders and parents can pass on to their pupils and children are known as *mana*. There is great responsibility here, as the teacher must test the pupil's sincerity and the pupil must test the teacher's true competence. The ancient Hawaiians did not pass on material things (at most, a canoe or cult objects); they primarily handed down *mana* – particular abilities and mental strength. This intangible legacy is worth far more than mere material goods, as material wealth can easily be lost, while you can always earn money with your knowledge and your abilities; economists call this *earning power* and/or *earning ability*, the power to transmute learning and expertise into hard cash. The blessings you receive from your forebears are the secret of the fourth commandment, to honour your father and mother, that your days may be long upon the land – it is the only one of the Ten Commandments with guaranteed healing properties.

The three selves – the inner family

The psychology of *huna* contains a model that is similar to the Western notions of subconsciousness, consciousness (the waking state) and superconsciousness. These are known as the three selves: the lower self *(unihipili)*, the middle self *(uhane)* and the higher self *(aumakua)*. This triad represents an inner family, and just as a person is able to follow their path with confidence and happiness when they have a good relationship with their parents, a person's character and mind is stable when their inner family is in harmony. As a meta-physician would put it: 'It's the same on the inside as the outside.'

Unihipili – the lower self, subconscious and inner child

Unihipili is the lower self, the subconscious. It has an intrinsic guiding authority that works independently and needs no conscious control. In *huna*, this being is known as the inner child. According to *huna* lore, the lower self has three tasks, namely data storage (impersonal aspect), database management (personal aspect) and regulating unconscious bodily functions. *Unihipili* stores all conscious and unconscious memories – and all ancestral memories – in the form of genetic programming and cell memories. As in a giant library, every memory from your own and from former lives, every scrap of male and female ancestral programming, every belief, decision and early childhood trauma is carefully shelved and labelled as good or bad. In addition, your lower self can access the morphogenetic field and the collective unconscious. The librarian is termed the inner child.

The expression *unihipili* is made up of three root words that tell us a great deal about the psychological peculiarities of the subconscious. *U* is the representation of an independent being: the inner child. This manages all bodily functions without our conscious intervention.

This being is active day and night – the perfect servant – and yet at the same time it is wild and difficult to tame. Its powers are immense and once you have won its confidence you will be able to achieve almost anything.

The root word *nihi* indicates that our inner child is scared of punishment and so sometimes refuses to perform its duties. *Nihi* also means 'black sack' and shows us how deeply feelings of guilt, certain complexes and their causes (unconscious memories), patterns and ancestral programming can be hidden. All this of course happens with the intention of saving us from further pain. Traumatic experiences are in most cases linked with strong feelings of guilt, and even victims of violent crime and children that have been sexually abused often feel partially responsible. Many people in our culture have been habituated into believing (1) that they are guilty of something since birth and (2) that someone who is guilty deserves punishment: a psychological poison chalice. Every therapist knows how fatal it is simply to tip out the entire contents of the 'black sack' and then to have a look at how the pile of debris might be collected back up. Instead, all you can do is slowly try to win the confidence of your inner child and then broach the topic in a safe space. It is only when you have found success with one topic that you can move on to another. This technique represents *mahiki*, peeling an onion.

In translation, the root word *pili* means 'to stick to' or 'to adhere to'. Just like a little child that clings to its mother and always wants to know and learn things, the lower self sticks to the *uhane*, the middle self. Everything the middle self says or thinks about itself or others (the inner dialogue) is considered the truth by the lower self. Your conscious self is responsible for identifying truth, and chooses which truths are allowed to penetrate into the depths of the subconscious as an image of yourself and the world. You (the middle self) determine which labels are stuck on to memories. The things you believe deep in your heart (the subconscious) are the things you come to expect and, as a result, are what you perceive in your environment as well. This is very simple neural conditioning, known to brain research for more than 40 years – those who think in black and white have only one way of being happy.

Uhane – the middle self

The translation of *uhane* is 'self-speaking being'. We speak with and about ourselves and other people. The word 'person' comes from the Latin word *personare* and means 'to sound through'. This goes right back to actors in the Ancient World who would hold masks (either angry, laughing or sad) in front of their faces, and the sound that resonated through the wood and the caricature carved into it went to make up the 'person'. The particular characteristic of any person is their way of speaking, and the way you speak about others betrays your character and your spiritual maturity; this is exactly what *uhane* is – a being that 'outs' itself through communication.

It has been said that in the beginning was the word. The origins of the word 'word' are to be found in the Sanskrit root *vrit*, meaning 'mental impulse' or 'wave'. When we say something, it is as if we were throwing a stone into the waters of our lives, and every word is a ripple of thoughts that spreads out and shapes the shore. The way you speak to yourself will shape your body and the way you speak to people will shape your relationships. We manifest ourselves through language – *vrit*, the wave – and so every word has value.

Exercise

*An exercise to help you make contact
with your inner child*

Explore your feelings about the following statements:

You are guilty.
My opinion is the only correct one.
I know what's right.
I know you.

And now activate the light-filled side of your inner child with the following statements:

You are valuable.
I respect your opinion.
I thank you for the experiences we have shared.
You have extended my horizons.
I thank you with all my heart.

The same on the inside as the outside – from the inner family to the external family. It is our inner dialogue that makes us happy or sad and forms our self-image. We will often have adopted this dialogue from our parents: what your parents thought about themselves and what they said to you has in all likelihood become the truth about yourself. In much the same way, the lower self accepts our inner dialogue as truth: the image that you have of yourself *(ike)* and whatever you are currently focusing on *(makia)* will shape your inner dialogue.

Uhane is the conscious component of your personality, the part that acts deliberately and wilfully. You are the person who is responsible for you, and as a middle self, you take over the guidance of your lower self. In developing your conscious being, you are responsible for the weight you give events and for the inner dialogue that you choose and maintain. If you feel unwell (your inner child is unsettled), it is the job of the middle self to perform a *ho'oponopono* to offer apologies and to carefully take over guidance.

Exercise

An exercise in examining your own vocation and/or your life's dream

Lay out six floor anchors on which you have written the following words: (1) My vocation, (2) My abilities, (3) The higher self, (4) Me, (5) The lower self and (6) The world. The focus in this constellation and/or conference is on your vocation (1). Lay out all the other elements in the system in relation to this floor anchor and search the feelings of each representative position in turn. Now perform a *ho'oponopono* from your 'me' position (4), saying, for example: 'I'm sorry that I gave you (1) so little consideration. Please forgive me. I love you. Thank you.' or 'I'm sorry that I did so little to advance you (2). Please forgive me. I love you. Thank you.' Now gradually try to identify a healing resolution formation. Where and how are the three selves, your inner family, arranged in relation to one another? Where are your abilities, your vocation and the world?

Aumakua – the higher self

The higher self is, as it were, the ambassador of the Source, an observer, a benevolent companion and a friend. The higher self is also known as the higher consciousness, the higher soul and the cosmic intelligence. It is the source of inspiration. *Aumakua*, the higher self, governs our cosmic plan – it is a latent determination, a kind of obligation and responsibility to the whole (Sanskrit: *dharma*) perceived as a vocation inherent in every living being.

Exercise

An exercise about your inner family

Write down on three pieces of paper: (1) *Uhane* (me), (2) *Unihipili* (inner child) and (3) *Aumakua* (higher consciousness). Lay these sheets of paper out as floor anchors. Stand on each sheet of paper and use your feelings to explore every aspect of your personality, asking yourself:

(1) How does my lower self feel?
(2) How do I feel as a middle self?
(3) How does my higher self feel?

Record each of your answers in your workbook.

Forgiveness as the key

The highest goal of every human being is a state of happiness and inner peace. The greatest obstacles on the path to happiness are resentment, negative memories and a feeling of personal worthlessness. Surveys conducted by Stanford University have shown that a lot of people think that their own unhappiness is the fault of circumstances, politics, institutions, world events or other people. In such cases, they have identified a culprit they can make responsible for their own unhappiness. In other words, you find a particular person that you don't think much of but whom you expect to change so that you can be happy again. Well, good luck with that … .

Being happy is an attitude to life that is less determined by outside circumstances and more by inner qualities. It is a character trait – and to develop your character into a mature personality, you have to learn how to free yourself from the negative influences of the past. This is the only way to live a life full of strength and happiness in the here and now. In order to be happy, you have to learn to forgive. People with mature characters and social attitudes are in a position to take responsibility for their own lives and to forgive. By the same token, people who cling to past events with anger, sorrow and self-reproach are like people driving down a mountain who only ever look in the rear-view mirror, never where they are going; if you only look back, you will never see what is right under your nose.

In our lives, especially in our childhoods, things can sometimes happen that leave a deep wound – but life would like to heal you. The principle of life is healing, acceptance, reconciliation, love and forgiveness. When you cut your finger, life activates all your powers of self-healing to close up the wound. Wounds heal as long as you don't scratch them open again, but your negative memories will rub against such hurts; this is why it is best to transform these negative memories and to concentrate on your real goals. Ask yourself what you would like to feel and experience in the future.

Both as parents and as children, we have to be able to forgive – whether in school, in professional life or in a partnership. To be successful in life and to love life, you have to learn to forgive – and the same is true for love. In fact, if love were a cake, it would have the following ingredients: (1) the ability to overlook little mistakes and *faux pas* that don't hurt anyone and (2) the ability only ever to wish good things for other people.

There are three categories of people you have to forgive in life: (1) your parents, (2) everybody else and, finally, (3) yourself. Forgiveness, especially self-forgiveness, is not easy, but anyone can learn how to do it. Imagine how much peace there would be among people and in the world if individuals would only forgive themselves and one another. Forgiveness is a key – it's like a car key that you turn and the car starts. This is the way to achieve a mature character and to accelerate your personal development; forgiveness might even be the key to international peace.

You don't die from the snake bite,
you die from the venom.

Proverb from India

Two monks

Two monks from the Shaolin* order once journeyed into far distant mountains. They wanted to renounce the world entirely, give up fighting and do nothing but meditate. They lived for four winters and three summers in seclusion in a cave. During the fourth summer, they felt in their hearts a desire to rejoin the world, and so they broke camp and walked down into the valley. On the way, they met two robbers. The two robbers bowed, for they had recognised them by their clothing as monks from the feared Shaolin monastery. 'You have nothing to fear – we have renounced martial arts,' said the two monks in a friendly manner. Without further ado, the robbers drew their swords and struck the monks dead.

The story of the two monks shows that forgiveness does not mean tacitly accepting everything, as occasionally we have to stop someone in their tracks with all the means we are legally permitted. The single aim of forgiveness is to release us from the energetic ties (Hawaiian: *aka*) that bind us to the perpetrator and the deed. Instead of being blinded with hatred, we will perceive the many beautiful things that exist in our own lives. In a *ho'oponopono*, we work from the principle that everything in life has its own message and that obstacles can be both stumbling blocks and springboards. It is just a question of turning your attention to the goal *(kūkulu kumuhana)* and following the lead of every successful person: let's look at the solution and ask ourselves what we have learned and gained from this situation. Let us say 'thank you' from the depths of our loving hearts and at that very moment move from deficit to abundance.

....
* The Shaolin order is a Buddhist order of monks from China. The brotherhood's original monastery is on Mount Song in Dengfeng county and adherents are renowned for their fighting skillsl *(Shaolin kung fu)*.

Exercise

An exercise with floor anchors about forgiveness

You will need three floor anchors. Write (1) the name of a person that you haven't yet forgiven on the first sheet, (2) your own name on the next sheet and (3) the words 'Neutral observer' on the third sheet. Arrange all three sheets of paper on the floor in a way that feels right to you. Stand on each of the three sheets in turn and search your feelings. How do you feel and how do you see the world differently *(ike)*? What are you concentrating on *(makia)*? What degree of freedom do you have *(kala)*? Regain control of your own strength *(mana)* and now perform *(manawa)* a simple forgiveness ritual *(aloha)*: 'I'm sorry that I saw you as an enemy. I am also an enemy. Please forgive me. I love you. Thank you for this healing of all involved. Thank you for this transformation. Thank you for the miracle.' Now stand on all three of the floor anchors in turn and explore your feelings. How does the neutral observer see the forgiveness ritual?

Following a new formula

For no other reason than our Western cultural influences, there are many people who have been in mental chains since earliest childhood and harbour great feelings of guilt; these are compounded with feelings of culpability about everything they have done and everything they have neglected to do.

I ask you this: if we were to speak again in a year, how would you have had to lead your life during those twelve months in order not to regret a thing? How would you have to behave in order to be free and not to be your own biggest critic and judge?

130

Exercise

An exercise about self-love

Stand in front of a mirror and carry out a 1:1 family constellation with yourself, saying: 'I love you … (say your own name) with all my heart.' Repeat this sentence several times and smile for 30 seconds, as this is how long it takes for every cell in your body to receive the endorphin rush.

Installing a new life

Forgiveness allows you to leave the past behind you and start anew. This is like reformatting the hard drive of a computer or installing a new operating system. The old data are then backed up in the Akashic records* and have no further influence on our lives. *Ho'oponopono* is a powerful inner cleansing that allows you to free yourself of these old data, memories and restrictive beliefs. If you have loaded the wrong program or the hard drive is too full, you have to start a new program and delete old data. It's the same with a pocket calculator – if you want to tap in a new sum, you first have to press C to delete the numbers from the last calculation. Imagine yourself as a computer: your body or your brain is the hardware and your way of thinking is the software. Now imagine how all of your memories – conscious and unconscious – are stored like data on the hard drive of a computer. Your destructive thoughts, memories, prejudices and hurts from the

---

* The Akashic records are a kind of subtle 'Book of Life' in which every event in human existence is recorded – everything that has occurred, is occurring now and will come to pass in the future.

past have the same effect as viruses and trojans. They slow down your system, generate incorrect results and make the system crash. The anti-virus program is launched in *pule*, the connection. In *mahiki*, the discussion phase, all the viruses and trojans are then identified and the disruptive programs are quarantined by *mihi*, absolution, pardoning and forgiveness; the highest operating system, the Divine Source within you, can then delete all the viruses and trojans from your hard drive with the command *kala* and/or the words 'thank you'.* What remains is a record in the form of your pure experiences, but now these experiences can cause no more pain as you will see only the things you have learned and the things that have sheltered you from greater suffering.

---

* See 'A summary of the four stages of a family conference', p. 77–78.

An example

As we reach the end of this little book, I would like to pass on to you an example that once again demonstrates how we switch roles on the stage of life. It shows how helpful it is to approach something like a child, able to feel only what is really real, and how important order and sequence are in the make-up of things. We can see what great results can be achieved when we put things back in their proper order – and this is the aim of a *ho'oponopono* and of a family constellation. The following example might seem unusual to anyone who has never taken part in a constellation, but for just that reason we can learn so much from it.

Philip is twelve years old. He is from Croatia and he has been living in Germany with his mother Maria for the last five years. Maria and Philip's father separated eight years ago. She happily remarried four years ago and Philip and his stepfather have an excellent relationship. Philip regularly visits his biological father in Croatia during the summer holidays, although as the father drives a taxi during the day, he spends most of his time with his grandparents.

Maria has asked for a personal advisory appointment for herself and for Philip and we (my partner Andrea Bruchacova and I) arrange a constellation with them, with floor anchors and cuddly toys as representatives. The issue at hand is to improve the relationship between father and son. When Philip talks about his father, he describes him as poor, weak and backward, someone who doesn't have any money to top up his son's pocket money. It is apparent that Philip is generally suffering from the absence of his father and of his grandparents. There is a shadow over the heart of the child.

Philip has already taken part in constellations as an observer and knows the procedure. From a collection of soft toys, he picks out a small dog as a representative for his father and puts it in a corner. He places a floor anchor (a sheet of paper with an arrow on it for the direction of his gaze) in the middle of the room as a representative for himself. We ask Philip how his father feels. 'My father feels small and weak.' 'And how do you feel?' we ask him. 'I feel better, somehow, strong. Well, we do live in Germany.' – 'Is your father allowed to get closer to you?' – 'No.'

We then ask Philip to arrange two objects to represent his grandparents. He takes two sheets of paper, writes the Croatian words for granny and grandad on them and places them nearer to him. This creates a triangle with father, grandparents and Philip at the corners. 'How do your grandparents feel?' – 'My grandparents feel sad.' – 'What is your father feeling now?' – 'My father has to be a bit higher now – can we put the dog on a chair? My father thinks he is better than his parents – he looks down on them as they have achieved nothing in life.'

Can you already see the pattern here? Philip looks down on his father just as the latter looks down on his parents. Philip and his father believe that the previous generation have failed and thus weakened themselves. The energy, the mana, and the blessings from their ancestors are blocked.

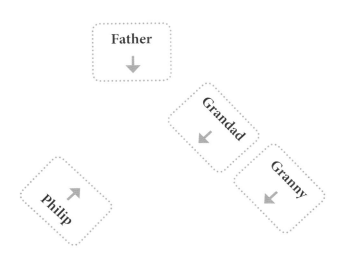

fig. 10

In the next stage, we shall bring order into the system and clarity to the chain of people. We ask Philip to go and stand in his father's place and say to the grandparents as a representative of his father: 'You are older and I am younger. You are my parents, and I am your son. I'm sorry that I looked down on you. Please forgive me. I love and respect you. Thank you.' We ask Philip to bow.

Philip now stands in the grandparents' place. Representing his grandfather, he says (as we are dealing with the father/son relationship here): 'I am your father. I am older and you are younger. I love and respect you. Thank you.' Philip explores his feelings in this position and says that his grandparents now feel strong and are glad about this good relationship. Philip would like to move his father and grandparents closer together.

Philip sits down on a chair as an observer of the constellation. We ask if his father is now allowed to come closer to him, to his floor anchor. He says yes. We move the chair and the dog closer. We ask Philip to stand in his father's place and, representing his father, to say to Philip's floor anchor: 'I am your father, and you are my son. I am older and you are younger. I'm sorry. Please forgive me. I love you. Thank you.'

We don't know what exactly is causing sorrow here, but Philip is bound to feel hurt in his heart at the separation of his parents. We want to resolve this in a simplified ho'oponopono. We ask Philip how his father is feeling now. Philip says that his father is feeling fantastic, adding that his father is now just as strong as his son. Before the constellation, Philip had felt bigger than his father, had partially looked down on him and had also adopted the position of his father in his relationship with his grandparents.

As the constellation facilitator, I now stand on Philip's floor anchor myself, so that Philip can distance himself from his own person and observe the solution in stages as an image. I say: 'You are my father, and I am your son. Life came to me through you.' There is a minute's silence. 'I had switched roles in the past. I'm sorry. Please forgive me. You are older and I am younger. I love you. Thank you.' We ask Philip if his father can come closer to him, and he welcomes the idea.

It is extremely helpful to collect feedback from the representatives when there are changes in the room. We ask Philip where the grandparents should now stand. Philip asks the grandparents to move closer as well. They are standing at a slight angle behind the father, but are easily visible to Philip.

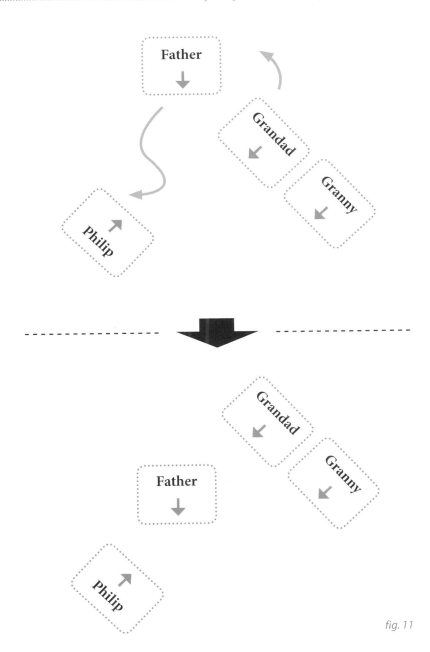

fig. 11

We ask Philip to stand on his floor anchor. He takes up position and bows. We have him say the following sentences aloud to his grandparents: 'I am your grandson, and you are my grandparents. Thank you.' He turns to his father: 'I am your son, and you are my father. I honour you and your life. I love you. Thank you.'

We ask Philip how he feels and he answers, 'Amazing!' We leave the healing resolution formation in place for a minute to take effect. We then clear away the floor anchors and give the dog and the other stuffed animals a shake; as a rule, representatives should pat themselves down or shake themselves out once they have stepped out of their role. We share another cup of peppermint tea and chat about the weather. I must admit that we were all very proud of Philip. The whole constellation had lasted only about 30 minutes.

A week later, Philip calls to tell us that his father has sent him 20 euros by bank transfer. 'It's the first time he's ever done it and it's a really large amount.' He says he is looking forward to the next long holidays with his father, and of course with his grandparents.

We often hear about life taking these unexpected turns, of healing in relationships with mothers, fathers, children, colleagues and employers, neighbours, houses and flats, with people themselves, with life and with much more. Healing does not always happen as quickly as in our example, but you still say thank you in a *ho'oponopono*: 'Thank you for the miracle. I can't see it yet, but I know that it is already on its way to me.'

Divide and connect – part 2

I was born under the sign of Capricorn, and if you believe in astrology you know that Capricorns are down-to-earth and practical people. Whether astrology is true or not, I am a practical person and am interested in what works. Because I am looking for happiness and peace, I try to be happy and peaceful. I don't always succeed but I am working on it, as it is well known that your real destination is the journey. If someone casually says to me that my destination is 'the journey', I occasionally answer that I am not interested in war, only peace – if I want peace, I must also follow the path of peace. My interlocutor will then begin to understand that the path and the goal must of course be in harmony. Peace on the outside can only be achieved with inner peace. External wealth is created through inner wealth. External unity and happiness is achieved through joyful and enthusiastic actions – by being happy in the here and now and not by waiting for the future.

All human beings are striving to be happy, and we are happiest when all our relationships are in order. This communion begins with loving interaction with ourselves, entirely according to the motto: 'Heal yourself and you heal the world.' The message of this and of all my books is thus a message of peace – inside and out. Indeed, I am entirely convinced that the great family of all living beings and our ecosystem (in other words, the house in which we all live) will come back into balance when we – you and I – centre ourselves again, turning our gaze to what connects us in our hearts, to the spiritual Source, and overcome the divisive ego: *nana I ke kumu* (Hawaiian: look to the Source).

A dog recognises its master whether the latter is wearing swimming trunks or a suit, has a wig on or has shaved off his beard, has donned a boiler suit or is completely naked. A dog recognises its master – always. By the same token, when I fail to see that the spiritual source in every living being is the same, wouldn't I have to admit that I have understood less than lots of dogs? But to err is human. When we become aware that there is something in our hearts that connects us with one another, that connects us for the very reason that we are different, we give this something various different names: the universe, an all-pervading intelligence, love, the Source, Krishna, Jehovah, Allah, God, Buddha, *ke akua*, Vishnu …

So let us follow the path of peace, all together and yet as individuals. Family constellations and *ho'oponopono* may be of use to you in such endeavours, and with all my heart I wish you great joy with these two tools, which will help you heal your relationships on every level.

Wishing you every success on your spiritual journey,

Ulrich Emil Duprée

Appendix

The Hawaiian family conference in detail

Traditional *ho'oponopono* consists of twelve steps and is divided into four sections:

(1) Opening phase, with a prayer and identification of the problem.
(2) Discussion phase, with a description of the perceptions, viewpoints, feelings and reasons for the behaviour.
(3) Release phase, with heartfelt mutual forgiveness and the release of all negative feelings.
(4) Closing phase, with a prayer and thanks to all involved for having chosen harmony and love. We simultaneously reinforce our common goal, and then we eat together.

These four sections are like the seasons and the individual steps correspond to the months. Mary Kawena Pukui emphasises that *ho'oponopono* is not an isolated concept but rather always represents the totality of *pule, mahiki, mihi* and *kala.*

4 phases   **4 seasons**   **12 steps**
4 sentences   **4 variants**   **12 months**

My question about the meaning and rightness of the different variants of *ho'oponopono* was answered for me by Hawaiian priest Haleaka Iolani Pule (the great-grand-niece of Morrnah Simeonah), who died in 2014. She said, 'All the variants are like leaves on a tree. The leaves are not the tree. *Ho'oponopono* is about healing relationships.'

Pule – the prayer

Ho'oponopono begins with an appeal to the ancestors or the Source. This prayer lays a powerful foundation for a successful start. All those present are lifted up to a higher level of energy. Prayers are one of the *kahuna* sciences and are the essence of shamanic *ho'oponopono*.

People use this prayer *(pule)* to ask for assistance, understanding, proper listening and correct speech. You ask for the strength to speak without hurting or blaming others. Much as in violence-free communication, people speak of their own perceptions, personal feelings and individual needs. You ask for the strength to hear and understand others: 'Without filtering it through my hurt, what is he or she saying?' You ask for the strength to express the truth, so that all concerned can understand what you would like to say. You ask for the seriousness of the situation to be recognised and for a chance to restore harmony. You give thanks for this opportunity to be close to one another in understanding and for being allowed to give and accept love. You give thanks for the power of forgiveness. You ask for wisdom, understanding, attentiveness, courage, truth and intelligence.

Kūkulu kumuhana

Kūkulu kumuhana is considered the warm-up phase. All the participants are brought on board as a team, as it were, and all resistance to the process of restoring harmony is rejected. The object of the exercise – wishing to resolve the individual or group problem in a loving way – is summarised and reinforced. *Kūkulu kumuhana* are the group's targeted good wishes and blessings for all the disputing parties.

Hala and *hihia*

Hala consists of identifying the specific problem. Someone might perhaps be looking for help with personal problems, with conflict at school or in their professional life. There may have been a breach of an agreement, an offence against some rules, unfulfilled expectation, misunderstandings or a crime. Whatever the circumstances, *hala*, the underlying problem, is often almost impossible to pin down, and so *hihia* are directly linked with *hala*. *Hihia* represent the various levels of the problematic issue, its effects and the many aspects of its expression in our interpersonal 'imaginations' (the images we believe to be true: he said that she said… and that's why…). Everything that disturbs, annoys or confuses us is a sign that we are not at peace with ourselves and that something has to be put right within us.

Anyone who has ever taken part in a family constellation will know the many dimensions an energetic blockage can take and be aware of its destructive effects across space and time. In other words, *hihia* welcome you to the realm of illusion, to the world of imagination, frustration, insatiable desire, misunderstanding, patterns, reactions and negative beliefs. The full scope of the problem could be compared to an iceberg: *hala* is the tip, the visible conflict, while the *hihia* under the surface represent the hurt and suffering of your ancestors and all those involved. Participants and observers may also be *hihia* within a conflict.

Mahiki

A problem always becomes visible on a number of different levels, and the phase of discussing this is known as *mahiki*. Here, you speak about what you see, hear and feel, outlining your own needs and those of the group in relation to agreements, expectations, wishes, hopes, goals, causes and effects. This conversation is a process of self-discovery; all those involved look into themselves and seek out their true motives. *Mahiki* is self-critical – no one is accused or judged. You will ask yourself: 'What are the actual root causes of my feelings and actions? What have I done or neglected to do? What have I done or neglected to do that has made me a part of the problem?' *Mahiki* literally means 'peeling an onion', and as layer after layer of these traumas are revealed, a lot of tears will be shed.

Mana'o

Mana'o is the phase in which all the participants are asked to outline their feeings, motivations, emotions and needs in a factual manner, so that everyone involved is able to get an idea of how the events that have happened came about. *Ho'oponopono* places the focus on the group and on shared experience.

Ho'omalu – time out, looking into oneself

Using abuse, emotional blackmail and verbal or physical violence in your dealings with others is a sign of powerful inner trauma. Things can get heated as frustration mounts (the result of unfulfilled expectations or wishes). At this point, *ho'omalu* is called – a time of peace, reflection and internalisation. Strength is created at rest. Understanding grows when you learn to express yourself comprehensibly, in a calm manner. Our common goal is harmony and not the pursuit of personal desires. Harmony can't be faked and it isn't created through some kumbaya-and-fluffy-bunnies mentality, it is sought through the awareness that creative co-existence is possible; synergy follows entirely naturally.

Mihi – mutual forgiveness

Mihi refers to words spoken with certainty, straight from the heart. It involves admitting that you have done something 'ugly' and destructive. *Mihi* represents the inner struggle to restore peace and clarity by asking for forgiveness. *Mihi* means to forgive, and whenever people ask for forgiveness, forgiveness is given. This is mutual pardoning and forgiveness. *Mihi* is carried out in three stages: (1) absolving on a material level, (2) pardoning on an intellectual level and (3) forgiving on a spiritual level deep in your heart.

Absolving includes settling any debts. This is the physical, material part in which the culprit gives back money or other items and/or arrangements are made to pay back debts and make amends. In a simplified *ho'oponopono*, we say 'I'm sorry' here, as it is understood that both parties have suffered. When we combine a family constellation with *ho'oponopono*, we bow at this point and say 'I'm sorry.'

Forgiveness now follows. Victim(s) and perpetrator(s) have understood what caused people to act harmfully and what needs they were trying to fulfil. These dysfunctional strategies, misunderstandings and incorrect behaviours are mutually forgiven. In addition, all the participants forgive themselves – without self-forgiveness, the *ho'oponopono* will remain incomplete.

The third stage concerns the heart. The participants say 'please forgive me' to one another, and the rule in a traditional *ho'oponopono* is that forgiveness is granted to all who ask for it – cleansing of the relationship is otherwise impossible.

Kala and *oki*

Kala follows from *mihi*. As soon as forgiveness has been asked for and granted with heartfelt sincerity on both sides, all negative thoughts are released. *Kala* means 'freedom', as all the negative ties that bind us to one another (the sticky bonds of *aka*) are separated. *Kala* means freeing yourself of all destructive emotions from that moment on, wasting no further thought on judgement, revenge, resentment, envy, etc. *Kala* means that we set ourselves free from the past. It is a process of transformation that reaches its climax in *kalana*, the moment of release. The situation and the problem are now *oki*. *Oki* means 'dealt with'. Once *mihi* and *kala* have been completed, the problem is over and is considered resolved. There is no further need to dredge up the problem. The hard drive has been reformatted. The problem is now with God, who has taken care of the transformation.

Pani

Pani is both a final restatement of the issue in respect of its solution and a reinforcement of the final goal of the individual or the group. What use would a *ho'oponopono* be if all those involved were to carry on behaving afterwards as they had done before? *Pani* translates as 'to stir' and here it means that the participants are all cooperating, all pulling in the same direction rather than pushing and tugging against one another.

Pule ho'opau

Pule ho'opau is the closing prayer. These are thanks to God and the ancestors *(aumakua)* for having granted all the participants understanding, intelligence and wisdom so that they were able to make an active contribution to the solution.

Communal meal – *aloha*

A traditional *ho'oponopono* is brought to a conclusion by sharing a meal, as this is a special expression of *aloha* and a good starting point for common goals and undertakings.

Useful lists

Feelings and emotions with negative connotations

abashed
absent
abused
agitated
alarmed
angered
annihilated
annoyed
annoying
anxious
appalled
argumentative
ashamed
belittled
belligerent
bitter
bored
cold
concerned
confused
constrained
constricted
contrite
cut off
dead
deceived
depressed
derided

deserted
desperate
despondent
difficult
disaffected
disappointed
disconcerted
discouraged
disenchanted
dismayed
displeased
disturbed
downcast
drained
driven away
dull
embarrassed
enraged
envied
exasperated
exhausted
exploited
fearful
fidgety
flustered
forbidding
forced into a corner
frozen

frustrated
furious
gloomy
grumpy
guilty
harassed
hate-filled
helpless
hesitant
horrified
hurt
ignored
ill-at-ease
impatient
incensed
indifferent
indignant
inhibited
intimidated
involuntary
irate
irritable
irritated
lethargic
listless
lonely
manipulated
meek

misconceived
miserable
misunderstood
neglected
nervous
not considered
not heard
not respected
not seen
not supported
not taken seriously
not understood
not valued
offended
overcome
overlooked
overstretched
panicked
patronised
perturbed
petrified

provoked
racked with cares
racked with doubt
rejected
repulsed
restless
rigid
sabotaged
sad
shocked
shouted at
shy
slapdash
sorrowful
strained
stressed
stupid
swindled
taken advantage of
tense
threatened

tired
trembling
unappreciated
under attack
under pressure
uneasy
unhappy
unimportant
unmoving
unsatisfied
unsettled
unwell
unwilling
upset
used
weak
wearied
worthless
wounded
wretched

Feelings and emotions with positive connotations

amused
astonished
attached
attentive
awake
balanced
beaming

blissful
blithe
calm
captivated
cared for
carefree
casual

certain of victory
charmed
cheerful
clear
collected
committed
composed

confident
considerate
content
cool
cosy
courageous
curious
delighted
determined
devoted
eager
easy
effervescent
emotional
energy-filled
enterprising
enthusiastic
excited
expansive
exuberant
fascinated
filled with love
fit
free
freed
friendly
frisky
fulfilled
funny
glad
happy
heeded

heedful
honoured
hopeful
impartial
impressed
in a good mood
in love
inquisitive
inspired
jubilant
light-hearted
lively
loved
loving
measured
motivated
moved
open
optimistic
overjoyed
overwhelmed
peaceful
peppy
perky
pleasant
popular
positive
powerful
protected
quick
refreshed
relaxed

released
relieved
replete
requited
respected
safe
satisfied
self-assured
self-aware
self-reliant
serene
silent
soothed
spellbound
stimulated
sure
surprised
tender
thankful
thrilled
touched
understood
unfussy
untroubled
useful
valuable
valued
vigorous
vital
well looked after
wide awake
zealous

Glossary

Aka (Hawaiian): rope, net

Akua (Hawaiian): god, goddess, a
supernatural being

Aloha (Hawaiian): love, divine
respect, compassion

Atma (Sanskrit): the self, the spirit

Aumakua (Hawaiian): ancestors,
gods of the ancestors, the higher
self, messenger of the gods

Blema (Greek): to throw

Chakra (Sanskrit): subtle energy
centre, link to the glands

Dharma (Sanskrit): duty, calling

Ha (Hawaiian): breathing out, life,
four

Haku (Hawaiian): a mediator/
companion in a *ho'oponopono*

Hala (Hawaiian): mistake,
misdeed, *faux pas*, error

Hana (Hawaiian): task

Hihia (Hawaiian): entanglement,
net, entangled participant,
eye-witnesses

Ho'o (Hawaiian): to cause, make

Ho'omalu (Hawaiian): time
out, period of silence, peace,
protection

Ho'omauhala (Hawaiian): being
unable to forgive

Ho'oponopono (Hawaiian): putting
things right again

Ike (Hawaiian): consciousness,
observation

Kahuna (Hawaiian): priest, one
possessing special knowledge, an
expert in *huna*

Kala (Hawaiian): to release, set
free, untie

Kalana (Hawaiian): freedom

Kanaka makua (Hawaiian): a
mature personality

Kanaloa (Hawaiian): a person who
walks with God, a great healer

Kane (Hawaiian): person

Karma (Sanskrit): the law of cause
and effect

Ke (Hawaiian): definite article
(the)

Ke Akua (Hawaiian): the Source,
the god in human hearts

Ki (Hawaiian): life force

K kulu (Hawaiian): to stack up

Kumu (Hawaiian): cause, source,
tradition

Kūkulu kumuhana (Hawaiian):
targeted good wishes from
the *ohana*, a blessing in a
ho'oponopono

La'akea (Hawaiian): divine light

Lei (Hawaiian): circle

Mahiki (Hawaiian): to peel away
layers, discuss

Makia (Hawaiian): attention

Makua (Hawaiian): parents, ancestors

Mana (Hawaiian): energy, life force

Mana aloha (Hawaiian): love energy

Mana Loa (Hawaiian): light energy

Mana mana (Hawaiian): energy of the will

Manawa (Hawaiian): moment of strength

Manu (Hawaiian): the great father of mankind

Mihi (Hawaiian): mutual forgiveness, pardoning

Noo noo (Hawaiian): consciousness

Odem (Hebrew): divine breath

Ohana (Hawaiian): family, clan, tribe or family-like group

Oi'a'io (Hawaiian): the absolute truth, the spirit of truth

Oikos (Greek): house

Oki (Hawaiian): finally letting go of a conflict, no longer heeding something

Pani (Hawaiian): stirring, summary, a shared meal

Peutein (Greek): to serve

Piha pono wai wai (Hawaiian): the law of abundance

Pilikia (Hawaiian): stress, problem, tragedy, drama

Pono (Hawaiian): right, flexible, mercy

Pule (Hawaiian): connection, prayer

Theos (Greek): god, goddess, a supernatural being

Tutu (Hawaiian): teacher

Uhane (Hawaiian): the speaking self, the middle self, the waking consciousness

Unihipili (Hawaiian): the lower self, the inner child, the subconscious

Wai wai (Hawaiian): life as a flowing stream of material and spiritual wealth

Acknowledgements

I bow before God, creation and all my teachers past, present and future. In this book, I would particularly like to thank the historian Dr Sebastian Diziol, the systemic constellations facilitators Myra Maas, Hildegard and Alexander Schwaan, and my systemic constellations teacher, Isolde Böttcher. My special thanks go to my physical and my spiritual family, and I owe a great debt of gratitude to Andrea Bruchacova and the entire team at my publishers, Schirner Verlag and Earthdancer.

About the author

Ulrich Emil Duprée is a spiritual researcher and teacher, author and seminar leader who has studied and trained in psychology, philosophy, huna, yoga sciences and metaphysics. His former homes have included a Hindu monastery, where he studied ancient Sanskrit scriptures.

www.Heile-dein-Herz.de

Picture credits

Decorative designs: lalan: palm leaf;Transia Design: sun; SPYDER: flowers next to the page numbers. All shutterstock.com.
Photography: Galyna Andrushko: page 8, 13, 35, 141; Maridav: 14, 88; naluwan: 44; pogonici: 54/55; Radoslaw Lecyk: 69; Dhoxax: 70; Yuriy Kulik: 82; Jack Haefner: 87; Romolo Tavani: 93; Berkomaster: 101; Evgeny Atamanenko: 120; Willyam Bradberry: 133; savitskaya iryna: 135; djgis: 142; Nadezhda1906: 145; Preto Perola: 147. All shutterstock.com.

Ulrich Emil Duprée
Ho'oponopono
the Hawaiian forgiveness ritual as
the key to your life's fulfillment
Paperback, full colour throughout,
96 pages
ISBN 978-1-84409-597-1

Consult our catalogue online (with secure order facility) at
www.findhornpress.com
Earthdancer Books is an Imprint of Findhorn Press.
www.earthdancer.co.uk

EARTHDANCER

A FINDHORN PRESS IMPRINT